Essays
on Puritans
and Puritanism

Essays on Puritans and Puritanism

by
Leon Howard

Edited by
James Barbour
and Thomas Quirk

UNIVERSITY OF NEW MEXICO PRESS
Albuquerque

Library of Congress Cataloging in Publication Data

Howard, Leon.
  Essays on Puritans and Puritanism.

  Bibliography: p.
  Includes index.
  1. Puritans—England—Addresses, essays, lectures.
2. Puritans—New England—Addresses, essays, lectures.
3. England—Church history—17th century—Addresses,
essays, lectures. 4. New England—Church history—
Addresses, essays, lectures. 5. English literature—
Early modern, 1500–1700—History and criticism—
Addresses, essays, lectures. I. Barbour, James.
II. Quirk, Tom, 1946–   . III. Title.
BX9334.2.H69   1986   285'.9   85–28878
ISBN 0–8263–0877–5

Chapter eight originally appeared in *The Huntington Library Quarterly* 9 (1) (February 1946): 149 and is reprinted with permission.

Contents

v

Foreword

Best known as an authority on Herman Melville, Leon Howard (1903–1982) wrote widely in the fields of English and American literature. His early articles, however, dealt mainly with early American literature, and he returned again and again to the subject throughout his life. He was working on a study of English and American Puritanism when he died. He had completed at least the first part of the work, a "History of English Puritanism." This volume of Leon Howard's writings contains the first and only completed section of the book, as well as a number of writings (including two previously unpublished essays) that deal with the subject of Puritanism and its influence upon the literature and culture of England and America.

The first part of the book, the "History of English Puritanism" (probably a more grandiloquent title than Leon Howard would have chosen), contains three chapters, each divided into three sections. Chapter 1, "The Background of Reformation," deals first with the social history of Europe during the Reformation, then isolates in part 2 the basic issues of Protestantism (giving brilliant, concise definitions of what is meant by the two fundamental doctrines: "justification by faith alone" and "the sufficiency of the Word"). He also sketches here the directions that disagreements over doctrines would take in the future of Protestantism. In part 3, Howard traces the course of English religious history through Henry VIII's reign to Edward's death in 1555 and to the 39 Articles of 1562 (the official doctrines of the Church of England).

Chapter 2, "The Church Puritans," deals primarily with the developments in England during the reigns of Mary and Elizabeth. In part 1, however, Howard calls attention to the models of church government abroad and to the fundamental issues raised by the Marian exiles in the Frankfurt church in 1554, where in two weeks the Marian exiles encapsulated in miniature the issues that would, over seventy years later, "divide English protestantism into two warring camps, Anglican and Puritan." In part 2, he explains the important role of the pamphlet *Admonition to the Parliament* (1572), and in part 3, outlines the position of the Brownists and the significance of the Martin Marprelate tracts.

Chapter 3, "The Release of the Word," begins with a brief history of the English translations of the Bible, explaining why the "aggressive" Geneva Bible was regarded as a Calvinist work and why it became the most popular bible of its day. In part 2, he traces the rise of preaching and psalm-singing and the development of the English Book of Common Prayer. And in part 3, he explains the attractions of Peter Ramus's dichotomizing logic to the Puritans and traces the development of the Puritan sermon form.

Professor Howard's approach combines historical analysis with a rereading of the basic documents. His brilliance lies in his ability to single out the most fundamental issues of theology and of church discipline in the history of Puritanism and then, by analyzing the basic documents, to explain how the key sixteenth-century writings affected the fundamental issues. He read all the scholarship, but he increasingly based his research primarily upon his own readings of the basic documents. He did not complete the book on English and American Puritanism that he intended to write. What we have in his "History of English Puritanism" is approximately the first quarter or (at most) the first third of the book. The apparent simplicity of his chapters belies his mastery of the subject matter, his uncanny ability to identify the most important topics for examination, and his expert presentation of the most complex materials.

The second part of the book consists of the William Andrews Clark Library seminar paper of 1958 on the *Puritans in Old and New England*. It helps explain what made him return to the study of Puritans after he had become the standard biographer of Herman Melville and one of the greatest authorities on nineteenth-century American literature. He hoped to account for "the apparently paradoxical fact that Independency in church government was a 'liberal' movement in England" but that in America it "was conservative from the beginning and became almost completely reactionary, leading to an active persecution of the sects and the enforcement of a death penalty against Quakers." His answers to this question were tentative, but they were based upon wide reading in the primary sources and upon an extensive knowledge of the civilizations of England and of America from the seventeenth century to the present. He asked to "be forgiven for suggesting that what I see or think I see in the literature of these early Puritans is a divergence in thought which was to develop into the basic difference between the English and American conception of government as it was gradually taken over by the people and institutionalized in the world's two most stable democratic forms." Both the modesty and the impulse to dare to ask the most important questions concerning the relations between literature and society are typical of Leon Howard. Could he have been able to give a more definite history of the relations between church government and the developing secular governments during the course of the seventeenth and eighteenth centuries, I suspect he would have tried. And I know that his attempts to answer such questions would have provoked admiration and reconsiderations from other scholars.

In his disarmingly and deceptively simple *Literature and the American Tradition* (1960), Leon Howard showed in his first two chapters how the Ramean logic of the seventeenth century and the Cartesian logic of the eighteenth helped create the different kinds of literatures produced in those centuries and helped create the different kinds of societies then existing. He had an extraordinary appreciation for the role of logic (which, in combination with memory, constitutes the primary ingredient of identity) in literature and in life. The third and final part of the present book consists of four essays showing how the new Ramean logic affected literature and life. Perry Miller and Father Walter J. Ong have both dealt with Ramean logic, Miller in his great volume *The New England Mind: The Seventeenth Century* (1939) and Father Ong in his study of the dissemination of the Ramean logic and the influence of printing upon conceptualization, *Ramus, Method, and the Decay of Dialogue* (1958). But no one else has shown the effect of Ramean logic upon literature as clearly as Leon Howard. Even after the work of Professors Hardin Craig, Perry Miller, Rosamund Tuve, and the earlier publications of Walter Ong, some excellent students of English literature could deny that Ramism really affected literature. (See George Watson, "Ramus, Miss Tuve, and the New Petromachia," *Modern Philology* 55 [1958]: 259, and his references.) But Leon Howard demonstrates the effect of Ramism.

The final four essays in the present book show, in detail,

how logical systems affect the underlying structures of literature. Leon Howard examines the role of logic in different works by Shakespeare, Thomas Cartwright, and Milton. Of his daring analysis of the logic of Hamlet's soliloquies, Howard wrote: "My own position, as I see it, is that of the innocent beholder who is perhaps sticking his neck out too far in an effort to see something new beneath the surface of one of the most ambiguous, intellectually teasing, and variously interpreted masterpieces of literature." Not so innocent as he pretends, though the modesty is certainly there, for Leon Howard knew that every act of speech is founded upon patterns of discourse that have been, whether formally or informally, learned by the subject. The scholar who thinks that Hamlet is not speaking in accordance with some patterning of logic and rhetoric is the real innocent.

In the unpublished essay on Ramean hermeneutics and the commandment against adultery, Leon Howard shows how the Puritan minister Thomas Cartwright used the Ramean "Arguments" in systematic scriptural exegesis, "and so provided the rationale for a number of Puritan practices in appearance, behavior, and attitude for which there were no specific injunctions." As Howard points out, these doctrines that Cartwright spun out of the seventh commandment "became incorporated in Puritan manners and custom and some of them into the sumptuary laws of the Massachusetts Bay Colony." Thus did a Puritan minister's keen application of Ramean logic become the social history of the following generations.

The previously published essay on Portia's reasoning in *The Merchant of Venice* analyzes the three roles and three different kinds of reasoning in her famous speech. The accompanying unpublished note deals with the use of Ramean logic in legal cases, with Howard pointing out that lawyers and judges were far more concerned with causes than were theologians. The last essay in the book was published in 1944 and is by far the earliest of Leon Howard's writings contained herein. More than any later piece, it shows him battling the contemporary critics. In this classic essay, he maintains that scholars have misjudged and misinterpreted Milton's *Paradise Lost* because they have ignored the underlying logical structure of that masterpiece. It is the standard article on the logic of *Paradise Lost*, cited by Father Ong in *Ramus, Method, and the Decay of Dialogue* and by every Miltonist since 1944 who is concerned with the underlying structure of that great English epic.

The present book moves from a description of society in the European Reformation to the significance of Puritanism for England and America, to the relevance of the particular forms of logic (and rhetoric) for literature and life, and finally to the ways that logic creates the literature and the society in which we live. If one asks, how was Puritanism important? Leon Howard supplies, better than any other scholar, a series of answers to that question. If Leon Howard had completed his book on English and American Puritanism, I believe that it would have grappled with such questions as the influence of Puritan and Anglican models of church government upon the development of modern political institutions and the influence of Ramean logic upon subsequent (especially upon American) literature and culture. But what he did, in the completed parts of the projected book as well as in his other books and essays, is certainly more than most of us could possibly hope to accomplish. And yet, when he thought of himself, it was not as a major scholar of his time, but as a teacher. And that was the purpose of his works—and will be the primary achievement of this collection.

As it stands, the book constitutes the best introduction to English and American Puritanism, to the fundamental issues in Puritanism, and to the implications of Ramean logic that we have. Every scholar who teaches early American literature will want to supplement this book with a survey of the major crises, the doctrines, and the most important individuals in the history of American Puritanism; but for the backgrounds of American Puritanism, for the application of Ramean logic to literature, and for the possible implications of the importance of the study of Puritanism, no teacher could do better than to send his students to Leon Howard's thoughts—and to read them himself.

University of Delaware   J. A. LEO LEMAY

PART ONE

History of English Puritanism

CHAPTER ONE

The Background
of Reformation

I

The Puritan movement was a peculiarly English phenom-
enon which grew out of the situation created by the desire
of Henry VIII to take over the Church of England without
reforming it and the willingness of his Archbishop of Canterbury, Thomas Cranmer, to keep up the appearances of
a Catholic church while making it Protestant in doctrine.
Each left his heritage: Henry to his equally strong-willed
daughter, Elizabeth, who was determined to preserve the
Establishment; and Cranmer to a series of successors who
were willing to accept the forms of the Establishment despite pressures from more zealous protestants to make the
Reformation in England as complete as it was on the Continent. Early in Elizabeth's reign the zealots had been con-
temptuously called "Puritans," but by the end of the
sixteenth century their persistence had rescued the term
from contempt and given it a definable meaning with reference to church government and morality. Later it was to
acquire doctrinal connotations and become the aggressive
label of a political party.

Yet the religious zeal of the seventeenth century—though
it was to produce civil war in England and a cultural pattern in America—was no more than a residual inheritance

from the turbulent century which preceded it. The sixteenth century was one in which the continent of Europe
was turned inside out. The discovery of America and of
an eastern sea route to the Orient—to be followed, during
the century, by the discovery of an Archangel route to
Russia—revised the commercial geography and began a
revision of the power structure of the Continent. Venice
was no longer queen of the seas, and its vast commercial
empire collapsed. The crossroads cities of Italy, the trading
cities of the Rhone and the Rhine were losing their power
and their glory as commerce took to the high seas. The
German cities of the once powerful Hanseatic League became ordinary towns when the Baltic became an inland
lake. Europe began facing outward rather than inward.
Antwerp became the commercial capital of the world, and
England, once a farming country on the periphery of trade,
found itself in the geographical position of its vanguard.

It was a century of inflation, social change, and popular
unrest. The gold and the silver of the Indies, pouring into
Spain, made bullion cheap and drove commodity prices
up all over Europe; and the government of England, knowing nothing of monetary theory and considering the mint
a "holy source" of revenue, debased the coinage to get
additional income to meet rising expenses. People were
suffering everywhere and beginning to desert the land and
move into cities. In Germany an effort was made to keep
them on the land by compulsion, and the result was a
bloody peasants' uprising in 1524. The English tendency,
despite the government's effort to control it, was the re-
verse. The new interest in trade made cloth manufacturing
the great business of the century, and landowners found
it more profitable to enclose their holdings for the pastur-
age of sheep than to keep them in cultivation. Farmers
became weavers or joined the growing mass of unem-
ployed. There were popular rebellions in the English coun-

tryside, too, but they accomplished nothing to stop the drift toward the city where the guilds of artisans were now falling into the hands of the wealthier members and the distinction between employer and employee was becoming as distinct as that between landowner and tenant.

It was also a century of political chaos. The Holy Roman Empire of the Hapsburgs was divided into two parts—Spain and the Germanic countries—and between them was France, ruled by the crafty and ambitious Francis I. He and the Emperor Charles V were at war in Italy for the control of its various provincial states, and Charles was at war with the invading Turks and finding it difficult to control the semiautonomous Germanic cities and states. England had possessive footholds in France, and France had a political foothold in Britain through its influence in Scotland—England's traditional enemy to the north. As the Holy Roman Empire went to pieces, Spain, the lord of the Indies, grew in its own power. Throughout Europe there was an intense spirit of nationalism. The smaller countries and larger cities wanted to preserve or gain their independence from imperial or foreign control, and the larger countries wanted to gain power and territory by any means at their command—by political marriages, by bribery and trickery, or by force of arms. England in the time of Henry VIII experienced both obsessions: the desire for independence, which tended to keep it united and stable at home; and the desire for foreign possessions and influence which kept it perpetually at war and insolvent.

The Roman Catholic Church, which had been a force for unity and stability in Europe, had little control over events in these changing times. No longer the intellectual citadel it had been in the time of Thomas Aquinas, its power of belief had been weakened by William of Ockham and a century and a half of his successors; and it badly needed the internal reformation later to be undertaken by the Council of Trent. Charges against the corrupt life of its clergy were widespread and well documented. It had been weakened politically by internal struggles for power and by its long conflict with the secular Empire. Twice at the beginning of the second quarter of the sixteenth century Rome was plundered by the armies of Catholic princes—first by the soldiers of Cardinal Pompeo Colonna, and a year later by the Spanish and German troops of Charles V under the leadership of the Duke of Bourbon. Nothing went unviolated, the papal palace, monasteries and nunneries, or St. Peter's itself. Accustomed to secular power and as hard pressed financially as any of the secular rulers, the Holy See had been trying to raise funds by the sale of indulgences; and it was against this active campaign for the remission of sins, for money, that the Reformation was first directed.

Martin Luther began it on Halloween day, 1517, when he posted his theses against indulgences on the door of the university church in Wittenberg. They were designed as a challenge to Friar John Tetzel, who was supposed to preach the new indulgences for rebuilding St. Peter's at the Wittenberg festival of All Saints' Day. But the particular challenge was not accepted. The Elector of Saxony had inadvertently taken his first step toward reformation by refusing to let Tetzel cross the frontier. The news of Luther's action, however, spread through Germany, and Luther himself followed it up with powerful sermons against the pretensions of the Church in standing between man and his eternal salvation through faith and the Word of God. Rome tried to suppress him, but his eloquence was unsuppressable without the cooperation of the German princes. At first the princes were neutral. Then they became protective. The Reformation gathered momentum and swept the Germanic part of the Holy Roman Empire with the encouragement of petty rulers who had no love for their Catholic emperor.

In the meantime a more radical Reformation began in Switzerland where Ulrich Zwingli, whose reformed views were already advanced, was called to Zurich and began expounding the Scriptures chapter by chapter and drawing from them doctrines opposed to most of the Roman teachings and practices. The theses he defended against a representative of the Bishop of Constance in 1523 were wide-ranging, and the decision in his favor by the Great Council of the city led to a complete reformation of the Zurich churches. They were stripped of their images, a vernacular service was introduced, the Lord's Supper was celebrated (in a radically new form) as a ceremony rather than a sacrament, and by 1527 a synodical form of church government was effected. By the time of Zwingli's death in 1531 the Zurich example had been followed by the cantons of Bern, Basel, St. Gall, and Appenzell; and the northern Swiss Reformation was far more advanced than the one still going on in Germany. It was entirely independent of the Lutheran Reformation and never came to terms with it. Luther considered Zwingli too radical in his doctrines and in his simplified forms of worship, and Zwingli was too severe and proud to compromise literal understanding of the Scriptures with Luther's evangelical emotionalism.

These primary reformers were helped by others: the scholarly Melanchthon, who rationalized and systematized Luther's teachings; Henry Bullinger, who succeeded Zwingli at Zurich and tried to carry on his work in a less severe way; the gentle Martin Bucer in Strasbourg, who was the first of the ordained priests among the major reformers to marry and who kept his associations with Luther and Melanchthon while following the examples of Zwingli and, somewhat later, John Calvin. These were the major leaders from whom the early English reformers were to seek advice and guidance in spiritual and ecclesiastical matters.

Had conditions been different a century and a half earlier the English reformers would have needed no advice from abroad. For their own countryman, John Wycliffe, had preached most of the doctrines of the sixteenth-century Reformation, led an active protest against the abuses and corruptions of the Church, translated the Bible into English for popular use, and gained a great and rebellious popular following. But Wycliffe had no printing press to spread his English version of the Word and his explications of it and no secular authority to support his reforms. Instead, his followers, the Lollards, were put down in one of the bloodiest repressions of rebellion in the history of England, and severe laws were passed against them and kept in force during the sixteenth century. Underground Lollardy may have played its part in the English Reformation—as it certainly did in the rise of various sects—but its public survival was in literature through the person of Chaucer's poor priest who could find a sufficiency in little and was loath to curse for his tythes and through Piers the Plough-man who could envision all the charities which are still considered worthy of tax exemption.

The new conditions which were apparently necessary for the Reformation may be found in the pattern which was followed everywhere. Spiritual leaders arose but required secular support and protection against the dual power of Rome. They got it because freedom from Rome not only meant spiritual and political freedom but freedom from the steady drain of money out of a country through the financial perquisites of the Holy See. It also meant, as the German princes were quick to see, an immediate gain of capital. For the material pattern of the Reformation, quite roughly and with many variations, was for the secular government to get the monasteries and the reformers to get the churches. The former were of no use to a new religion which depended upon preaching and had an evangelical suspicion of any retirement from worldly affairs. The latter provided the pulpits, and a major problem of the Reformation was to become the question of who was entitled to use them. From the beginning the decision was often left to the civil authorities, and when state supremacy began to be preached as a doctrine by Thomas Erastus this solution became known as Erastianism. But a good many old prejudices on this subject survived, and a good many second thoughts were to occur.

Within this general pattern, the procedure of reform varied from country to country. Luther had no great interest in ecclesiastical organization and did not insist upon uniformity. As an evangelist working with the people he cast off the bishops instead of converting them, and Germany and the Low Countries abandoned the principle of apostolic succession and the authority that went with it, developing a system of church government by conferences or synods representing the individual churches of a city or state. In Sweden, when Gustavus Vasa won independence from Denmark and demanded the confiscation of church property as a condition for remaining on the throne, the whole church was taken over and the bishops adopted Lutheran doctrines. When the Reformation reached Denmark that country adopted the Lutheran term *superintendents* for its ruling ecclesiastic but soon transformed them back into bishops.

At the other extreme was the Swiss system, especially as it was to develop at Geneva. Switzerland was not a nation, and its jealous cantons, each dominated by a single city, were not inclined to develop a national church. Nor was Swiss democracy inclined to continue the forms of an episcopal hierarchy. Geneva was peculiarly independent, on the defensive, and alone. Achieving its independence in 1536 after only four years of Reformation, it was a small city of less than ten thousand souls walled against its Catholic neighbors and militantly devoted to the Protestantism which symbolized it and enabled it to preserve its freedom. Three months after its citizens had voted unanimously to "live henceforth according to the Law of the Gospel and the Word of God, and to abolish all Papal abuses" their spiritual leader, William Farel, recruited the twenty-seven-year-old John Calvin to help him build the church which would preserve their unity.

Calvin did not begin to acquire power, however, until he had spent three years of exile in Strasbourg and returned in 1541 to a city which was not only independent but relatively free from the political and religious influence of Bern; but within the next fifteen years, by the force of intellect, character, and conviction, he had become controller of a city of refuge and inspiration for French and Italian Protestants. When the English immigrants began to arrive in 1553, they found a City of God which was ruled by the Word: civil authority was vested in a Small Council of twenty-five *Messieurs* (who called the church pastors and selected the elders), a larger Council of Two Hundred, and an occasional public Assembly of citizens. Ecclesiastical authority was vested in a Consistory of pastors and elders. No man's ministerial authority was superior to any other's, but Calvin's interpretation of the Word was persuasive enough to make sure that all things were done "decently and in order." Geneva, in the opinion of John Knox, was "the most perfect school of Christ that ever was in the earth since the days of the apostles."

Because Geneva had been a center of trade rather than of learning and because of its position as a city of refuge on the southern frontier of Reformation, its churches were truly international in their outlook. None of the ministers in the four French language churches was a native, and

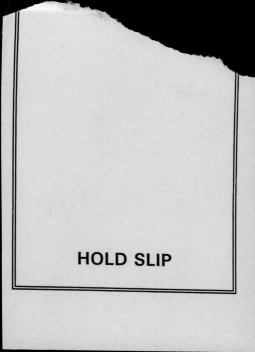

HOLD SLIP

the Italian, English, and Spanish congregations were, of course, served by ministers from their own countries. They lived together in conformity to the Word, as Calvin interpreted it, and sent out well-trained preachers and (after the great influx of printers during the fifties) books to spread it. More than any other city, little Geneva became the great international center of Protestantism.

II

However closely connected the Reformation may have been with the political and economic turmoil of the sixteenth century it was instituted and carried on by men who were more concerned with the life to come than with the world about them. Two great convictions dominated their minds and fortified their emotions. The first, formalized as the basic Protestant doctrine by Martin Luther, was a belief in "justification by faith alone"—i.e., a conviction that faith in God was the only thing necessary for a man to achieve a certain degree of saintliness in life, the salvation of his soul from the fires of hell, and the achievement of perfect holiness in a state of heavenly accord with God's will. It placed Luther and all other Protestants in complete opposition to the Roman Catholic Church which considered itself the divinely ordained mediator between sinful man and a merciful God. The second, an article of faith rather than a formal doctrine, was a belief in "the sufficiency of the Word"—a conviction that the Word of God contained everything necessary for man's guidance along the road to salvation. Since this, by implication, denied both the authority and the dogma of the Roman Church, it was as obnoxious to Catholicism as the doctrine of justification by faith was heretical.

Each of these convictions had complex and far-reaching

implications. The first placed man in a direct relationship
with God. The only mediator between the two had been
Christ, and if a man, by the grace of God, was one of those
for whom Christ had made his sacrifice, he needed only
to believe in Him to have everlasting life. It was this doctrine which gave Lutheranism the evangelical and emotional quality that enabled it to sweep Germany. If the
Church had no control over man's fate after death, its
practices were superstitious, its corruptions could be denounced, and its impositions could be avoided. Yet man
could not earn grace any more than he could purchase it
from the Church, for the power of faith was itself a gift
from God. The doctrine thus made the good works advocated by the Church as spiritually indifferent to Protestants as its practices were unnecessary. In his efforts to
achieve faith a man could only seek for an awareness of
grace and so discover his duties in life and prospects for
eternity.

The Protestant denial of the saving efficacy of good works
opened the door to the many antinomian sects which were
the rabble of Reformation, but the followers of Luther,
Zwingli, and Calvin were believers in the Law and in the
practice of piety. They simply made a distinction between
"justification" (which was a technical term referring to a
man's spiritual state as having been accounted or judged
righteous and therefore ready for heaven) and "sanctification" which referred to the process of becoming saintly
or spiritually perfect. The first was a judgment of God,
mercifully given through his grace. The second could never
be wholly achieved on earth or achieved in heaven without
justification. Yet imperfect human evidences of an earnest
and active desire for sanctification might be a sign of one's
spiritual state. No conscientious Protestant could avoid the
obligation to be zealous in good works, nor could he be
complacent about them.

"Faith" was an equally technical but more difficult term. It normally implied both an act of knowing in the form of perception and belief and an act of volition in the form of trust. It was particularly difficult because it was used in various senses in the New Testament, the words of Jesus usually placing emphasis upon the act of trust and those of St. Paul emphasizing belief. Catholic doctrine not only placed its stress upon the notion of trust but eventually reduced faith (insomuch as the ordinary layman was concerned) to an acceptance of the authority and dogma of the church. But to Luther, as to St. Paul, faith was a perception and belief so vital and active that it became a force in itself, available to anybody who experienced the grace of God, which could regenerate mind and spirit by direct apprehension of Christ through the Word of God. It freed him from the authority of the church and the mediating power of the sacraments (although he allowed them a certain secondary importance) and put him in an immediate relationship to the Divine Being whose Word he could study and to whom he could pray. Calvin and his followers also felt this immediate relationship through faith but were more disposed to stress their trust in the revealed Word while they searched it over and over again and created a structure of belief more systematic than any the Lutherans required.

Despite all the variations that existed within it, the doctrine of justification by faith alone put the Protestants in direct opposition to the Catholic doctrine of being judged righteous by merit—whether this merit was acquired through mysterious sacramental channels or through obvious works of charity and piety. The Protestant was expected sincerely and earnestly to repent of his sins, not to do penance for them. His faith and hope were supposed to lead to a feeling of love, not to acts of charity. The Lutherans were so willing to keep the sacraments for their

secondary value and were so convinced that faith produced good works that their practices sometimes confused
more severe Protestants. But this was not to occur until
some of the philosophical implications of justification by
faith alone had been explored by John Calvin and his followers who raised new doctrinal problems.

These problems were created by the concept of predestination which was implicit in the doctrine of justification
by faith alone. If individuals were to be accounted or judged
righteous before they achieved sanctification—if they could
not be saved by their own efforts or those of a mediating
priest—how could they be saved? The answer regularly
given by Protestants was by God's grace, freely granted
to those whose sins had been expiated by Christ's sacrifice.
This was a doctrine which could be readily held by those
who had acquired strong convictions—who had experienced faith—that they were chosen by God for his holy
purpose. Its first effect was to provide firmness of purpose
to the Protestant leaders who were aware of their human
frailties and convinced that they must overcome them in
the service of a divine cause. It was also a source of evangelical zeal because the first service to the cause was the
awakening of others to an awareness of God's grace. For
a person who might expect to be burned alive before he
was resurrected to eternal bliss, this might be as "sweet"
a doctrine as the English Articles of Religion said it was
two centuries before Jonathan Edwards was to offend pos-
terity by describing it in the same way.

The belief in personal "election" to salvation, as it came
to be called, created no serious problems until the Calvinists began to dwell upon the complementary notion that
those who were not of the elect must necessarily be "rep-
robated" to eternal damnation. But this was to come later,
after the publication of the 1559 edition of Calvin's *Insti-
tutes*. The early years of the Reformation were years of

discovery—of man's new relationship to God through faith and through the Word—and of zeal in rallying God's chosen people to the cause of true religion. The basic doctrine of Protestantism had to be taught and accepted before it could be refined and purified.

What faith was to the spirit, the Word was to the mind and heart. All Protestants agreed that it was a sufficient substitute for the Church as a guide to salvation and that it should be made widely available. But it, too, was a technical term with a variety of meanings. There was common acceptance of the Scriptures as the revealed word of God, but within the Scriptures the word of God was sometimes the law of the prophets or the teachings of Jesus, sometimes an inspiration such as came to John Baptist in the wilderness, and sometimes the divine being ("the Word made flesh") in the person of Christ himself. Luther found the authority for his Reformation in the Scriptures and was the first reformer to translate the whole Bible from the original Hebrew and Greek texts into the vernacular. But in his preaching and to a certain extent in his translating he was inclined to find more authority in what he considered the spirit of Christ than in what was literally written down. Zwingli and the Swiss school generally tended to look upon the Bible as a book of laws and instructions, complete in itself and to be supplemented only by inferences to be drawn from the practices of the primitive church and the teachings of the earliest fathers. The question whether "the Word of God" meant simply the Bible or something inspirational or spiritual which did not go contrary to the Scriptures was a question on which the German and Swiss reformers were divided from the beginning and one on which the English reformers were to split in the course of time.

Nevertheless "the sufficiency of the Word," however interpreted, was a basic Protestant tenet because it stood clearly opposed to the Catholic doctrine of the efficacy of the sacraments. Both the Eastern and the Roman Catholic churches maintained that souls were saved from eternal damnation through seven sacred rites of the Church: baptism (which admitted new believers and the children of believers into the fellowship of the Church), confirmation (which conferred upon them, after they had reached the age of understanding and discretion, the full privileges of the Church), the Eucharist (or supreme act of worship, in which the communicant actually partook of the body of Christ), penance (the act of repenting, confessing, atoning, and receiving absolution for particular sins), matrimony (which sanctified the union of man and woman), holy orders (through which the power of the Church was handed down to the priesthood), and extreme unction (which involved anointing the bodies of those who were in danger of death and praying for their souls). Protestants kept only the two sacraments, baptism and the Eucharist, or the Lord's Supper, as they preferred to call it. They abolished penance and extreme unction (and along with them the doctrine of purgatory and private masses for the dead) as contrary to their basic doctrine. But they tended to preserve matrimony and the admission to holy orders as solemn if not sacred ceremonies, and, except for those extreme sects which denied the propriety of infant baptism, they substituted for confirmation periodic examinations of the worthiness of individuals to participate in the Lord's Supper.

The Protestant rejection of the sacraments other than baptism and the Lord's Supper was based upon an inability to find them contained in the Word—that is, in this instance, clearly authorized by the Scriptures. The two authorized sacraments, however, created serious differences among the Protestant groups because the Scriptures were not clear about the nature of the rites and what was involved in them. All of the major reformers accepted the Catholic practice of infant baptism and at least that part of the rite which required sprinkling with water. Some extreme groups, though, maintained that there was no precedent either in the Scriptures or in the primitive churches for infant baptism and held that true baptism involved a spiritual rebirth which was possible only for mature believers and should be performed by total immersion. This belief was an old one, but it was publicly debated in Zurich and other Swiss cities with the result that a second baptism was made illegal. The Anabaptists, as the members of these groups were called (for at this time almost everybody who was baptised in maturity was baptised anew), were considered heretics in most countries because they denied the efficacy of the traditional sacrament; and this division among the Protestants became the most serious of the Reformation.

The Eucharist or Lord's Supper caused much more sophisticated differences of opinion, but it seriously affected Protestant unity because it determined which churches could communicate with each other through the mutual participation of their members in this communion service.

The Catholic doctrine, against which all Protestant groups protested, was that of transubstantiation. It held that at the time of their consecration in the Eucharistic mass the bread and wine were miraculously transformed into the real substance of Christ's body and blood. Whether substance was understood with the medieval scholastics as that universal essence which is found in every particular or whether it was understood in the gross and literal sense accepted on faith by the vulgar, it made the priest (or the Church through him) the instrumentality in bringing Christ to the people and making possible their union with him. In doing so, it made impossible the close personal relationship between God and man which was implicit in the doctrine of justification by faith alone, and it also made the works of man a necessary step toward justification. The two doctrines were incompatible, and their incompatibility was made even more evident by a Catholic theory (widespread at the beginning of the sixteenth century) that the sacrifice on the Cross had served to redeem man from original sin but that a repetition of the sacrifice in the Eucharist was required to redeem him from his individual sins.

The Protestants could readily agree in rejecting the doctrine of transubstantiation and the idea of priestly power implicit in it and also in rejecting the theory of the repeated sacrifice. But they could not agree upon a single doctrine to replace the Roman one. Luther developed the doctrine of consubstantiation, holding on to the idea of the corporeal presence (or Real Presence, as it was called) of Christ in the bread and wine but denying the miracle by saying that Christ existed in these elements before they were consecrated. But this involved him in a bitter quarrel with the Swiss reformer Zwingli who maintained that the Lord's Supper was a commemoration of Christ's sacrifice and that the bread and wine were merely signs or symbols. The followers of both were suspicious of Calvin and his followers who tried to hold a middle ground by maintaining that the sacrament was a real means of grace in that it strengthened man's spiritual union with Christ but that his presence was in the bread and wine only as a spiritual power or virtue.

There were also many differences of opinion as to the proper method of conducting the rite. Here again the Protestants had one common ground of protest: they protested against the Catholic practice of excluding the laity from the communion cup, reserving for the priests the privilege of participating in both the bread and the wine. "Communion in both kinds" became a Protestant symbol, like clerical marriages, which marked the progress of the Reformation without regard to the basic doctrines of salvation. Some of the other symbols in the elaborate ceremony of the Mass were reformed because of the doctrines associated with them and others independently, but the most significant of the Protestant practices were those directed against the adoration of the Host—especially in refusing to kneel and in the substitution of the communion table for the altar.

During the period of the English Reformation these were the questions that tried men's souls. Ambitious men might scheme for the Church's possession or play politics with religious forces abroad. But honest and earnest men—and there were many of them—died for their beliefs.

III

The separation of the English church from the church of Rome was not in itself an act of reformation although it placed the new Church of England in the secessionist group and made it subject to strong Protestant influences. These influences had already begun to trickle into the country when underground Lollards learned that their secret opinions were openly held and openly practiced in "Almany" across the sea. One of these was actually arrested and charged with singing and another with speaking the praise of Luther. In more sophisticated circles Luther's doctrines were being discussed within a few years after they were formulated. A group of Cambridge scholars began meeting at the White Horse Inn (locally referred to as "Germany") as early as 1521, and by 1525 there was a strong suspicion of Lutheranism at Oxford—which became a center of distribution for Lutheran literature until its secret scholar-bookseller was arrested in 1528. London merchants were in close contact with Antwerp (where they protected William Tyndale in the "English House" until he was betrayed) and other cities; and bookselling was good business—especially after the appearance of Tyndale's translation of the New Testament into English in 1526. There were also antiRoman laws on the English statute books, not in force but ready to be used, and widespread resentment against Cardinal Wolsey and his grandiose style of living. But England did not produce a reformer of the continental type.

The reason is to be found in the king. Henry VIII was a powerful personality who came to the throne when Englishmen still remembered the terrible civil war of the Roses and were anxious for the internal peace that might be secured by a strong monarchy. Henry himself had no sympathy for Protestant doctrines and took pride in the title Defender of the Faith which he had received from the Pope for his defense of the sacraments against Luther's attack in *The Babylonian Captivity of the Church*. Staunch as he was in doctrine, however, Henry was not willing to be politically subservient to Rome. He needed a male heir to preserve the strength of the English monarchy, his queen Katherine of Aragon was unable to produce one, and his fancy had settled upon Anne Boleyn as her successor and the possible mother of a prince. He wanted a divorce. For years, with surprising patience, he sought one. But for part of that time the Pope was captive to the Emperor Charles V (the Queen's nephew, who was not at all averse to seeing his cousin Mary in the position of being the sole heir to the English throne) and was in no position, then or later, to grant one.

While the negotiations for the divorce were going on Henry acquired two new advisers—Thomas Cromwell, a favorite of Wolsey who had maintained his influence after the cardinal's fall; and Thomas Cranmer, a Cambridge divine who had volunteered a suggestion that the divorce question might be settled by the universities of Europe rather than by the papal court. Cromwell was a blacksmith's son who had been a soldier in France, a banker in Italy, and a merchant in Antwerp before becoming one of the most learned lawyers in England. He was able, efficient, and ruthless; and he was thoroughly convinced that Henry would be one of the greatest princes in Christendom if he were free of Rome and had the riches of the English church at his disposal. He was familiar with Machiavelli's *The Prince*, with Marsiglio of Padua's arguments in favor of a secular head for the church, and with the events of the continental Reformation. Cranmer was willing to flout Rome and was developing, in his cautious way, Lutheran opinions. Twice married, he had already adopted Lutheran practices, and his second wife (1532) was the niece of a prominent Lutheran divine.

With a parliament which had already shown itself willing to attack the privileges of the Church and revive ancient statutes to control the clergy, and with Cromwell growing to a position of dominance in the Privy Council, Henry needed only to make Cranmer Archibishop of Canterbury in order to obtain an English divorce. The see had only recently become vacant, and papal bulls were necessary for Cranmer's consecration. But time was of the essence for a legal heir. Anne was already pregnant, and a secret marriage was performed in late January, 1533. The bulls arrived, Cranmer was consecrated Archbishop of Canterbury on March 30, and on April 23 a convocation of the English clergy annulled the marriage of Henry to Katherine on the grounds that the king's marriage to his brother's widow had been contrary to divine law. Anne was crowned on June 1, and the heir-to-be—though it would be Elizabeth rather than a son—was legitimatized.

This meant a complete break with Rome. It was made

formal by parliament early in 1534 by a series of acts designed to prevent any payments of tribute to Rome and
to require the absolute submission of the clergy to the king
and by a later Act of Supremacy which declared the king
the "only supreme Lord in earth of the Church of England." Henry became, in effect, an English pope. Although he controlled most of the administration of the
church through the Archibishop of Canterbury, Henry kept
its major reforms in his own hands by appointing Cromwell his vice-regent for ecclesiastical affairs; and Cromwell,
who was already Chancellor of the Exchequer, immediately undertook the expropriation of monastic properties
which was a regular part of the Protestant reformation.
The smaller monasteries were dissolved in 1536 and the
larger abbeys in 1537, and by 1540 the monastic orders—
the monks, friars, and nuns—had disappeared from English life. The properties which had supported them, together with their treasures of plate, went to the king, who
sold off much of the land to the newly rich and helped
hurry the rise of a landed gentry with a vested interest in
the new religious regime and in a monarchy strong enough
to control the old feudal nobility.

The assault on the monasteries gave encouragement to
the members of the clergy who were inclined toward Protestant doctrine, but they got no other encouragement from
the king. The Ten Articles of religion, devised by his own
majesty in 1536, set up the authority of the Bible in matters
of theological truth and denied the instrumentality of the
forms and ceremonies of the church in the remission of
sins. But they preserved the Mass and everything within
the church which did not contribute to the power and the
authority of Rome. A few months later they were followed
by a series of injunctions, issued by Cromwell perhaps
with Cranmer's encouragement, requiring the clergy to
preach twice a quarter against the authority of Rome, to

declare the Ten Articles, to distinguish between those necessary for salvation and those necessary for the decent and politic order of the church, and to see that children were taught the Lord's prayer, the creed, and the Ten Commandments in English. They also enjoined the clergy to refrain from encouraging pilgrimages and image-worship, from haunting ale-houses, and to care for the poor, encourage education, preserve their vicarages, and see that the sacraments were reverently administered. The Reformation was going as far as the Defender of the Faith would permit.

Even this much Reformation was not accomplished without popular resistance. There were uprisings in Lincolnshire and in the north, more against Cromwell than against the king, which were put down by force while procedures against the larger monasteries continued until the last of them was taken over by the crown in the spring of 1540. In the meantime the reformers were having second thoughts. "The Bishops' Book" of 1537, *Institution of a Christian Man*, was a compromise which restored the four sacraments not mentioned in the Ten Articles; and although Cromwell in 1538 ordered that the Bible in English be made available in every church, a counter-reformation was actually underway. The Six Articles of 1539, supported in person by the king and passed unanimously by the Lords and with only two dissenting votes by the commons, restored Catholic doctrine and practices in the church and made heresy and persistent non-conformity punishable by death. After Cromwell's fall in 1540 England was Catholic in every respect except allegiance to Rome.

The reformers, however, were merely waiting. Henry's marriage to Anne had been declared null after her execution in 1536, and he had immediately married Jane Seymour who gave him in October, 1537, the male heir he had so long wanted. The boy was being educated by Protestants, and Henry himself, toward the end of his reign, was aware that Protestant sentiment was growing in the country and had reason to distrust the Catholic party in his court. His will set up a predominantly Protestant regency for young Prince Edward, and Henry's death, on January 28, 1547, assured the beginning of another phase of the English Reformation.

It began with a step that Henry himself had planned because he needed money for his French and Scottish wars—a confiscation of the chantries and other endowments of the church, including guilds, colleges, and hospitals, which were not devoted to public worship. The Edwardian Act, however, was Protestant in its rationale because it was specifically directed against "vain opinions of purgatory" and masses for the dead (including those for Henry, which he had paid for in advance). It was also more comprehensive in that it included secular fraternities and guilds, although it was enforced only with respect to those funds that were used for "superstitious" purposes. Cranmer was more cautious than the young king's secular advisors had been. Though the Privy Council abolished all images in the church, he was anxious to achieve uniformity by compromising with the conservatives and was content at first with a new Order of Communion which simply introduced English prayers into the Mass and then with a Book of Common Prayer (1549) which was entirely in English but in English that he hoped would be ambiguous enough to make it acceptable to extreme Protestants as well as to those who were still of the Catholic persuasion.

With the fall of the Duke of Somerset, the king's uncle and Protector, the situation changed. The new Protector (who made himself Duke of Northumberland) had got the support of the conservative bishops and politicians in order to gain his office but immediately removed them from power, leaving Cranmer with a much freer hand. In the meantime the Archbishop had been getting strong support from abroad. Charles V had finally found time from his troubles with the French and the Turks to attempt a suppression of the Protestant Reformation in Germany and had forced the imperial states and cities to sign an interim agreement on a form of worship which appeared to foreshadow a return to Catholicism. Many of the people who refused to sign or accept *The Interim* found refuge in England, and among them were some of the most famous divines in Europe. But few of them were Lutherans. The scholars and preachers were of many national origins, but almost all of them came by way of Zurich, Basel, or Strasbourg. The teachings of Zwingli, Martin Bucer (who came in person and was made Regius Professor of Divinity at Cambridge), and Calvin began to be more discussed than those of Luther.

The results became evident in the second Edwardian Book of Common Prayer which appeared in 1552 and even more so in the Forty-two Articles of Religion which were published in the king's name in June, 1553. The Articles were not formally agreed upon in a London synod as the title page claimed, but subscription to them was required of everyone who held an ecclesiastical office or was licensed to preach or who became a candidate for any university degree. The young king's death, less than a month later, made them ineffective at the time; but when they were revived, revised, and reduced to thirty-nine in 1562 they were not to be greatly changed.

The Church of England, as established at the time of Edward's death and perpetuated by Elizabeth, was a reflection of Thomas Cranmer's sensitivity and ingenuity rather than any man's reforming zeal. The private and political interests of Henry VIII made his work possible, and the anti-Romanism of Cromwell, Somerset, and Northumberland enabled him to exercise his talents for compromise more freely than he could have if he had been in the vanguard of reform. The church reflected both the growing independence and nationalism of England and the internationalism of Cranmer's personal receptiveness toward new ideas. Its theology might be described as being early Calvinistic, up-to-date at a time before Calvinism achieved its later rigidity; but its forms were traditional, modified only enough to be clearly Protestant rather than Roman. Services were in the vernacular which protestantism everywhere demanded but were conducted from a traditional Prayer Book which preserved the dignity and the literary quality of its Catholic predecessors. It was neither Reformed Continental nor Roman but an English church.

Cranmer never satisfied such extreme Protestants as John Rogers, Hugh Latimer, and Nicholas Ridley; but when he went to the stake with them during the Marian persecutions two years later he had laid the foundations for a Church of England which their followers would try to purify but would never attempt to destroy.

CHAPTER TWO

The Church Puritans

I

Shortly before his death on July 6, 1553, Edward had willed the crown to the Protestant daughter of the Duke of Suffolk, Lady Jane Grey, who was immediately proclaimed Queen but quickly overthrown by Mary Tudor whose unquestionable legitimacy gained her the support of even so aggressive a reformer as Bishop Hooper. But Mary was a devout Catholic who first restored the church services to the forms used during the last year of her father's reign and then lent her Supremacy to the return of the English church to the jurisdiction of Rome. The married clergy were all deprived of their livings, and the leading reformers who did not go into hiding or exile were imprisoned. When the Plantagenet laws which permitted the burning of heretics were revived, the more prominent of them were sent to the stake. John Rogers was the first, on February 4, 1555, and was quickly followed by Bishop Hooper, John Bradford and others. Bishops Latimer and Ridley were burned in October. Archbishop Cranmer, whose flexibility had enabled him to establish the church despite all the vicissitudes of Reformation in Henry VIII's time, was imprisoned and persuaded to recant. But he publicly revoked his recantation and was burned in March, 1556.

Some of those who went into hiding formed secret congregations in England. Those who fled to the Continent
established English churches in Strasbourg, Frankfurt, Basel,
Aarau, Zurich, and Geneva—sometimes in association with
the foreign Protestant congregations who had been allowed to leave England. They acquired first-hand knowledge of certain aspects of the European Reformation but
were forced to live in poverty, existing on charity or supporting themselves by menial jobs. The news of Mary's
death, on November 17, 1558, and of the accession of Elizabeth to the throne came to them as a message of deliv-
erance and a call to battle.

Their battleground was to be the church, and they were
more conscious of the enemy than of their own aims. They
were united in only one conviction: that the Pope of Rome
was the Anti-Christ who had been responsible for their
exile and for the martyrdom of their friends. His influence
upon the Church of England must be utterly destroyed.
What would take the place of Catholicism the exiles were
not willing to discuss, despite the urgings of John Knox
and the congregation at Geneva, as they packed their mea-
ger belongings overnight in their haste to get home. The
reformation of doctrine, accepted by all the churches abroad
and established in the forty-two Edwardian Articles, they
took for granted. The reformation of the church, they seem
to have felt, would somehow be accomplished by a Protestant queen and the influence of the Word.

But neither the mind of the Queen nor the scriptural
Word was altogether clear. Elizabeth, who loved ceremony
and had preserved her inheritance by paying lip service
to Catholicism during Mary's reign, was in no hurry to
overthrow the old religion until she knew what would be
established in its place; and the Word revealed two quite
different churches which had been approved of God in
accord with quite different circumstances. The oldest of

these was a national church, designed to include a whole people in its membership and to re-inforce their nationality by the religious discipline. This was the church of Moses and the prophets and of the law. The other was the New Testament church of true believers, gathered together by faith in order to worship as best they might under adverse conditions. This was the Christian church, but it was a church which had existed when there was no such thing as a Christian nation. Most of the Marian exiles had been members of gathered congregations, worshipping in their own way under adverse circumstances, but their ways had been different. They had no common background of experience by which they could interpret the Word on the proper nature of a reformed church.

The experience of Englishmen, at home, with gathered congregations was of little use to the Reformation. The secret meetings of the Lollards and of the congregations of Anabaptists had always been and were still illegal, and those who participated in them had no direct influence upon the established church although they may have been an important part of the undercurrent of radicalism which became apparent in times of change. The only legal gathered churches were those tolerated for foreigners—refugees from the persecutions of the *Interim* in the middle of the century and foreign merchants and craftsmen who were welcome residents of England in its new period of industrial and commercial development. During the later years of Edward's reign there had been French, Italian, Dutch, and German congregations in England, with ministers speaking their own languages and services conducted according to their own forms. The most famous of the foreign pastors had been John à Lasco, the son of a Polish baron and the inheritor of Erasmus's library, who had come from Emden in 1548 to become superintendent over the four German and Dutch congregations in London and to set the first example in England of what was later to be called the Presbyterian form of church government.

The Protestant congregations which continued to gather during Mary's reign had no firm character because their very lives depended upon flexibility and secrecy. The London congregation met in a variety of places, in private homes, in shops, and on ships, and was served by a succession of ministers; and it was a truly "gathered" church of the primitive Christian sort, made up of true believers who were necessarily self-governing because their worship was outside the law. Yet they worshipped according to the Edwardian prayer book and tried to model their government on John à Lasco's church (which had disbanded on Mary's accession) by keeping in touch with other underground congregations and with their brethren in exile. There were others in various parts of England, some without ordained ministers, but the circumstances under which they existed were not such as to provide a model of organization which might prove attractive in more propitious times.

The models, for those who wanted them, came from "the best reformed churches abroad." These, within the experience of the English exiles, were mostly Swiss; and the Swiss churches, if not national, were territorial. The Zurich model, which was generally followed in northern Switzerland, was of a church which was subordinate to the civil magistrates but which achieved uniformity and discipline by means of regular conferences of the clergy in classes or synods. The Geneva model, however, was better known than that of any other single church because about one-fourth of all the Marian exiles, in the course of time, became members of the English congregation there. It had four types of officers: pastors, who were to be concerned with discipline, the administering of the sacraments, admonitions and exhortations, and teaching; teachers, whose specialized function was the interpretation of the Scriptures in the interest of pure and sound doctrine; elders, a council of "pious, grave, and holy men," whose responsibility was the correction of vices; and deacons, who administered alms and cared for the sick and the poor. Each was an officer of his particular church, but pastors were, on the authority of the Scriptures, allowed to help and consult with one another; and the pre-Roman primitive church provided precedent for their meeting together in a consistory with one officer presiding although all ministers (pastors and teachers) were equal in rank and dignity.

Civil government was separate from that of the church, but it had jurisdiction over both tables of the Ten Commandments—that is, it was responsible for the purity of religion enjoined in the first table as well as the moral law of the second. A good magistrate "who is the father of his country, and, as the poet calls him, the pastor of his people" was a blessing from God, but even a wicked magistrate should be obeyed because his office was ordained by God—unless he attempted to set himself above the "King of kings," for any command against Him "ought not to have the least attention." Geneva had been traditionally governed by citizens who were normally members of the church and subject to its supervision. Although they selected the church officers, the church kept a close eye on them; and the kind of supervision it exercised is revealed by the Genevan Service Book prepared by John Knox and approved by Calvin for the use of the English congregation. Each week the church officers were to gather together for the correction of their faults and those of the congregation and "if there be any covetous person, any adulterer, or fornicator, forsworn, thief, briber, false witness-bearer, blasphemer, drunkard, slanderer, usurer; any person disobedient, seditious, or dissolute; any heresy or sect, as

Papistical, Anabaptistical, and such like; briefly, what so ever it might be that might spot the Christian congregation, yea, rather what so ever is not to edification, ought not to escape either admonition or punishment."

The Geneva system, from 1555 to Calvin's death in 1564 and for some years under Theodore Beza thereafter, was a model that could never be copied and never forgotten. It was, in effect, a territorial church which was international in its aspirations toward absolute purity of religion according to the literal interpretation of the scriptures. It was evangelical in spirit, welcoming refugees and training preachers for service abroad. It was in the first years of its peculiar glory, of course, when the English congregation was established there, and John Knox called it "the most perfect school of Christ that ever was in the earth since the days of the apostles." Geneva was the timely model of a Protestant community created by a man who knew the Word and his own mind, knew how to make both clear to others, and knew that in times of upheaval and chaos it was desirable to add to the commandments of Moses and Jesus another commandment of St. Paul to the Corinthians: "Let all things be done decently and in order."

But the Protestant leaders returning to England had less need for models, had they only realized it, than for experience which would guide them in solving new problems; and the experience they could have used best had been obtained by many of them (including a substantial portion of the Geneva congregation) at the beginning of the Marian exile in the city of Frankfurt. For there, in miniature and in the short space of two weeks, they had uncovered the issues which were eventually to divide English protestantism into two warring camps, Anglican and Puritan, and later destroy the Puritan movement by splitting it into Presbyterian and Independent factions.

The first refugees from the Marian regime to arrive in

Frankfurt were members of the French congregation of Glastonbury weavers who, as foreigners, had been allowed to leave England as a group under the leadership of their pastor Valérand Poullain. There they were allowed the use of the Church of the White Ladies, and, when William Whittingham and other English refugees began to straggle in during the summer of 1554, they offered to share their church with their fellow exiles. The municipal authorities were agreeable on condition that the English should avoid dissension by accepting the French Confession of Faith and adopting an order of service which would not offend their hosts. The newcomers readily agreed and accordingly settled upon an order of worship which had little or no relationship to the English prayer book. They also provided for a strict control over church membership, requiring a confession of faith, submission to church discipline, and doctrinal and moral tests. And they adopted the organization of John à Lasco's London church with officers consisting of a pastor, preachers, elders, and deacons. The Frankfurt church was just about as "reformed" as any that was yet to be in Massachusetts Bay.

The Frankfurt congregation chose their own ministers by vote—first John McBray, and later John Knox from Geneva with Thomas Lever from Zurich as his colleague. All went well until the spring of 1555 when a new group of English exiles, led by Richard Cox, former Vice-Chancellor of Oxford and Dean of Westminster, arrived and participated in the services. Cox was offended by the new order of worship which had been developed in consultation with the other churches in exile and created a disturbance by oral responses to the minister as called for by the English Prayer Book. He insisted, when the elders protested, that he and his group would "have the face of an English church." Knox demanded "the face of Christ's church" but was willing to put the matter to a vote, and he used his influence to overcome the objections of his congregation and admit the newcomers to full church membership. They promptly voted Knox out of office. On the grounds that their preference for the English form of worship violated the agreement by which they were allowed the use of the church building, Whittingham appealed to the civil authorities who insisted upon the French service—until the Anglicans frightened them by accusing Knox of treason to the Emperor. Unhappily, they asked Knox to leave the city; and within two weeks after his arrival the Frankfurt church was in Cox's hands.

The affair at Frankfurt is of unusual interest because it brings into view the three conceptions of a church organization which were to trouble England for a century. When Cox and his followers arrived, the organization consisted of a voluntary gathering of the Elect, each convinced of his justification and capable of enduring a rigorous examination on the purity of his doctrine and morals. If it had been kept so, as a majority of the congregation apparently wished, some of the newcomers would not have been admitted because of an unwillingness to sign the discipline or pass the doctrinal test. But Knox wanted a more comprehensive church which would be territorial in the sense that it would include the whole community of believers although it would be international insomuch as he believed that Christ's true church would have the same face in every territory. And he was willing—perhaps influenced, at Frankfurt, by a combination of generosity and overconfidence—to modify the severity of its membership requirements in order to achieve it. The newcomers wanted a national church which would preserve its national peculiarities in a distinctive ceremony of worship. They were to have their way in England but struggle long with people of other views. John Knox was to have his way in Scotland, completely and rather soon. But two generations were to pass before the founders' way became the establishment of Massachusetts.

In the meantime Cox and his followers obtained permission to use the English service in the church at Frankfurt, and most of Knox's supporters (and several who failed to support him) followed him to Geneva. This physical division of the Frankfurt congregation, small as it was, became the first major division of the English Protestants. When the Geneva congregation proposed unity in seeking an Elizabethan establishment the Frankfurt congregation was the most firm in its refusal to cooperate. When Elizabeth eventually turned her mind, early in 1559, to a religious settlement, the committee selected to achieve that purpose included Richard Cox but none of the men of Geneva—and John Knox was not even allowed to enter England. Geneva became a symbol of the opposition during Elizabeth's long reign, and symbolism was to play an important part in the controversy which was to produce the Puritans.

II

None of the active reformers who came out of hiding or returned from exile at the beginning of Elizabeth's reign questioned the idea of a national church. The question was whether the Church of England would be modeled upon "the best reformed churches on the Continent" or whether it would preserve the ecclesiastical organization it had inherited from the church of Rome and the traditional forms and ceremonies which were Roman in origin but not based upon Catholic doctrine. And at first no one questioned the ecclesiastical organization. The queen and her most important advisers, William Cecil and Nicholas Bacon, were determined upon a secure and stable government; and the existing church hierarchy enabled the Queen (who was persuaded to call herself the "supreme governor" rather than the "supreme head" of the church, but who had no intention of giving up any authority) to control the church through the Archbishop of Canterbury and the convocations of bishops. The reformers were generally committed to the authority of the civil magistrate and certainly had no desire to jeopardize the power of the new Protestant magistrate in a predominantly Catholic country. Inevitably the first controversy concerning the nature of the English church centered upon those forms and ceremonies which were symbols of alliance with the Catholic church or the Protestant churches of France and Switzerland.

The Elizabethan settlement of 1559 gave no encouragement to the reformers. Even the carefully selected committee who proposed it, composed of men who had never left England and of exiles who were completely free from the influence of Geneva, were disappointed. Elizabeth herself insisted that the Act of Uniformity, passed in April 1559, require certain changes in the second Edwardian prayer book that would remove the petition for delivery from "the tyranny of the Bishop of Rome and all his detestable enormities" and the rubric which explained that the act of kneeling at communion did not imply adoration of the Host. She also insisted upon a restoration of the 1549 wording of communion service (which was ambiguous about the Catholic doctrine of the Real Presence) and upon the restoration of the clerical garments or "ornaments" used in the second year of Edward's reign.

Most of the changes in the new prayer book which offended reforming sensibilities were offenses of omission, designed to avoid disturbing the Catholics, who might be expected to shift their allegiance from the Pope to the Queen if they were not required to make a public renunciation of their most cherished beliefs. The restoration of the older ornaments of clerical dress, however, was a direct challenge to the more extreme Protestants because it required their public renunciation of the symbols of sympathetic affiliation with the best reformed churches abroad. Bishop John Hooper had made an issue of clerical vestments before his martyrdom, and the new Calvinists wore their plain black Geneva gowns as a symbol of their protestantism and perhaps of their belief in the equality of the clergy. The argument about clerical vestments centered upon the claim that these were among the "things indifferent" which could be established for good order in the church without affecting the conscience of the individual— a claim which all conforming Anglicans and many of the reformers abroad were prepared to accept. But some of extreme reformers held that they were not things indifferent because they had been touched by superstition, or that, if they were, they should be things indifferent to the church when it came in conflict with individual consciences.

Archbishop Matthew Parker tacitly took the latter position until the spring of 1564 when Elizabeth, now more concerned with appeasing Catholic than Protestant sentiment abroad, insisted that conformity in clerical dress be enforced. She would not lend her name to the effort, but her will was clear and Archbishop Parker was forced into a reluctant campaign to make the English clergy look alike in dress regardless of what differences they might hold in their opinions. He tried to reason with the intellectual leaders of the objectors and found them now convinced that the vestments were consecrated to idolatry and no longer "things indifferent" to a man of conscience. Bishop James Pilkington of Durham (who had demonstrated his sympathies the year before by making Whitingham his Dean) appealed to the Earl of Leicester to urge the Queen not to stir up a quarrel that might deprive the church of many learned and godly men who were badly needed in it. But Elizabeth was in a reactionary mood, stopping a sermon at Paul's Cross by shouting for the preacher to quit his attacks on images, and Leicester could not have influenced her if he had wanted to attempt it. Parker followed orders and, with the assistance of Grindal and other bishops, drew up a series of Advertisements which voided all existing licenses to preach and prescribed in detail the vestments to be worn by the clergy at various services.

Bishop Grindal had no inclination to enforce the new rules, nor did the Mayor of London want them enforced; and the Queen would not take the responsibility of giving the rules her official sanction and support. Both Parker and Sir William Cecil knew the Queen's wishes if not her mind, however, and Cecil backed Parker's order that the ministers conform. Several were deprived of their livings or forced to resign during the spring of 1565, and the commission decided to move in on the universities. Oxford, where the reformers were few but vocal, came first; and the commission succeeded in depriving Thomas Sampson of his deanship and sending him to prison— though only for a brief period. But they were unable to touch Humphrey, whose elective position was subject to review only by the Bishop of Winchester who was himself more anxious to negotiate conformity than to enforce it. Three bishops, in fact (Pilkington of Durham, Parkhurst of Norwich, and Sandys of Worcester), refused to deprive any of their clergy during the controversy.

But Parker kept trying. Cambridge was becoming the stronghold of reform, and St. John's college was in open rebellion while the students of other colleges were breaking windows and engaging in Protestant pranks. Both Cecil and Parker labored long before they could bring it under control. London, however, was the crucial city. The common people were unruly, the merchants were deeply involved in foreign trade with the Protestant countries in Europe, and all were under the jurisdiction of two bishops (Grindal of London and Horne of Winchester) who were known to be opposed to the strict enforcement of Uniformity. Parker summoned a meeting of the clergy on March 26, 1566, and called the roll, demanding of each a simple "yes" or "no" response on conformity. Thirty-seven (more than a third of those in attendance) gave negative responses and had their incomes immediately sequestered for a period of three months during which they could either change their minds or lose their positions permanently.

Although the conflict was to last for another year, it was not to be marked by the cruelty of the earlier confrontations of reform and reaction. Among the intellectuals it was a war of pamphlets, in which questions of legality and expediency were as important as questions of principle. The Queen stayed publicly aloof and received protestations of loyalty from both sides. Even the Scottish reformers, who were in the midst of a violent revolution against their queen (and who, for a while in the autumn of 1565, seemed likely to receive Elizabeth's support), tried to mediate the controversy by urging toleration upon the bishops; and so did the continental reformers, on the whole, who disappointed their English friends by supporting the bishops' arguments for expediency. In the end many individual cases of conscience were compromised, the printed controversy was lessened by an act to license publications, and an appearance of peace was achieved.

Yet the vestiarian controversy, superficial though it may have been in its symbols and arguments, reached depths that had not before been evident in the English Reformation. One was to bring under serious attack, for the first time, the hierarchy of the English church. No one

questioned the Queen's supremacy. To do so would have
been high treason, and she herself had been shrewd enough
to avoid inviting this by refusing to lend her name to the
Advertisements or to letters urging their enforcement. The
bishops took the blame and the abuse, and their office was
weakened (perhaps not entirely to the Queen's displea-
sure) as a result. Another effect of the controversy was to
emphasize and strengthen the national character of the
Church of England. Henry VIII had wanted catholicism
without the pope. The Edwardian reformation had established Protestant doctrine. During the reign of Mary the
tendency had been away from nationalism: she exercised
her supremacy only long enough to restore allegiance to
Rome while most of the Marian exiles were being con-
verted, without fully realizing it, to an international protestantism. Elizabeth insisted upon a church which would
be peculiarly English and, as much as possible, entirely
her own.

   If she could have had her way, it would probably have
been a church, more polarized than Cranmer's, which was
Protestant in doctrine and Catholic in form—and more
independently English because its doctrines would have
separated it from Rome and its forms would have separated it from the reformed churches on the Continent.
Although the Reformation had already gone too far for
this balance to be perfectly achieved, the church as it was
did provide, in a time of suspicion and spying, the means
for a loyalty test of Her Majesty's subjects; and it was used
as such throughout Elizabeth's reign. When her foreign
policy required that she appease the Catholics, she harried
the international Protestants by insisting upon conformity
in clerical dress and ceremonies; and when the Catholics
became a threat, she suppressed them, much more severely, by enforcing the supremacy and the acceptance of
doctrine. Her attitude was a puzzle and a torment to sin-

cere souls of any persuasion who wanted to see a "true" church established in England, but it was one that could have been readily shared if not created by such an adviser as Cecil who was soon to become Lord Burghley.

It was during the vestiarian controversy, when the reformers had been put into the position of protesting too much against what appeared to be a minor question of conscience, that the word Puritan came into being. It came from the Latin *puritani*, an equivalent of the Greek *cathari* who considered themselves holier than their fellow men and for that reason withdrew from the world. But it was also used as an equivalent of *precisionist* in reference to the English reformers' insistence upon precise Scriptural authority for all the forms and ornaments of the church. In both instances it was a term of contempt and a useful one to the Anglicans because its double implication associated the reformers with the Anabaptists and other sectarians who considered themselves too holy to associate themselves with the establishment. For a while the reformers resented it, but eventually they found it a challenge. They did want (as John à Lasco had publicly told the king of Poland as early as 1555) a church of "apostolical purity," and to get it they would have to purify the firmly established Church of England. The word had positive and active as well as captious connotations, and in the course of time it was to become the most aggressive political party label in English history.

But in the meantime the Puritan impulse was to languish until it found a more positive outlet than resistance to a required form of clerical dress. By the spring of 1567 most of the reformers (with the notable exception of the learned ex-bishop, Miles Coverdale, who died as poor as he was when he returned from exile) had conformed. Others, who were not able or influential enough to ease their consciences by the anticipation of future influence within the

church, became itinerant preachers who met secretly with
gathered congregations of the sort that had existed in Mary's
reign. They were threatened by the Queen, sought out by
the sheriff of London, and, when discovered, investigated
by the Ecclesiastical Commission which found one congregation so defiant that thirty-one of its members were
imprisoned. This was the beginning of a clearly defined
and lasting movement toward separation and an embar-
rassment to the active reformers who were critical of the
church as it was but who were devoted to what they hoped
it would become.

The Marian veterans, in any event, were growing old
and tired and were more aware than were the radical London citizens of what was going on abroad. There the Duke
of Alva was engaged in a murderous repression of the
Protestant Low Countries, and the French Huguenots were
engaged in a civil war. In Scotland the Catholic Queen
Mary had been deposed and the crown given to her infant
son James, under a Protestant regency, while she was imprisoned in England. Elizabeth sent arms and men to the
Low Countries and confiscated the Spanish gold in English
harbors which was on its way to pay the Duke of Alva's
restless troops. But she was afraid to encourage French
intervention against Spain because of the danger of losing
control of the North Sea. There were no French forces in
Scotland at the time, but the Catholic north of England
was in armed rebellion and was being put down by force.
It was no time for the Puritan impulse to be directed against
a Protestant queen.

Two events, however, soon gave the reformers more
securely Protestant ground to stand on. One was the excommunication of the Queen by Pope Pius on February
25, 1570, in an attempt to release all Catholics from their
obligations of loyalty, an act which the Catholic rulers on
the Continent did not support and which was kept quiet

in England until May when a papist was bold enough to nail a copy of the Bull of Excommunication on the Bishop of London's door. The other was the Ridolfi plot of 1571 to overthrow Elizabeth and place Mary on the throne, which led to the arrest of the last influential Catholic noblemen and the beheading of Norfolk, the last of the feudal dukes. The parliaments of 1571 and 1572 were both aggressive in their efforts to reform the church, especially in their efforts to improve the quality of the ministry, and were kept under control only by the Queen's determined insistence upon her own prerogative in ecclesiastical matters. But an appeal to parliament, whatever its powers may have been, was good propaganda, and this was the form taken by the first genuinely Puritan attack on English church government.

It appeared as a printed *Admonition to the Parliament* prepared by John Field and Thomas Wilcocks, two of the younger generation of reformers, who were probably advised by such older returned exiles as Anthony Gilby, Thomas Lever, and Thomas Sampson; and it probably was published before parliament adjourned in June 1572, although it was never formally submitted to that body. It demanded a revision of the Book of Common Prayer which would remove from it "all Popish remnants both in ceremonies and regiment"—i.e., changes in the forms and substance of the prayers, the abolition of the word "priest," the use of preaching instead of written homilies, the examination of communicants, the use of common bread instead of the communion wafer, simplifications of the sacrament of baptism and the ceremony of marriage, and the abolition of such Catholic customs as the "churching" or purification of women after childbirth, emergency baptism by midwives, and the observance of numerous holy days. It also objected to the injunction "receive the Holy Ghost" in the ordination of ministers, to the "popish" vestments, and to ministers who were either "mass-mongers," nonresidents, or pluralists holding more than one charge. All of these were the standard demands of the reformers which the new movement took over in connection with a radical attempt to purify the church with a thoroughness that few of the earlier reformers had dreamed of and none had dared attempt.

This was to be complete removal from the church of all those "lordly lords, archbishops, bishops, suffragans, deans, doctors, archdeacons, chancellors, and the rest of that proud generation, whose kingdom must down, hold they never so hard, because their tyrannous lordship cannot stand with Christ's kingdom"—in short, every minister whose position made him superior to any other minister—and with it the abolition of the Archbishop's Court (a "filthy quavemire"), the Court of High Commission ("a petty little stinking ditch, that floweth out of that former great puddle"), and the power of the clergy to hold civil offices. Instead the *Admonition* demanded "a right ministry of God and a right government of his church, according to the Scriptures set up" which would frankly be that of the "poor men" who were "slanderously" called "Puritans." It would be a church in which every minister had his flock, in which no minister would be ordained unless he had been chosen by a particular congregation, and in which government would be committed exclusively to the ministers (pastors and preachers or teachers), the seniors or elders, and the deacons who owed their positions to congregational election rather than to civil authority. Its discipline would be sustained not by the civil magistrate but by men "instructing and admonishing one another."

A prolonged controversy and a second Admonition was required to bring out all the implications of the first (for its implied restrictions upon the royal prerogative would have been treason if made explicit), but the appearance of this widely read address to the people, though in name of an appeal to parliament, marked a new and radical development in the English reformation. It accepted, however reluctantly, the Puritan label; and it was vigorously aggressive in its insistence that "it is not enough to take pains in taking away evil but also to be occupied in placing good in the stead thereof."

III

The controversy was many-sided. The *Admonition* was first answered by the Bishop of Lincoln in a London sermon which was in turn answered in a widely circulated manuscript. The secret Puritan press also issued a pamphlet exhorting the bishops to make a more formal answer, and Thomas Whitgift, master of Trinity College, Cambridge, was commissioned to do so. While he was preparing it a *Second Admonition* appeared in the autumn of 1572, and the controversy continued in manuscript replies to Anglican sermons and manuscript correspondence with the reformed divines abroad, Beza giving support to the Puritans from Geneva, and Bullinger and Gualter supporting the bishops from Zurich. Protestant feeling was especially high because of the St. Bartholomew day massacre of the Huguenots in France, on August 24, 1572, which the complications of English foreign policy had prevented the government from protesting.

The most carefully reasoned defense of the Puritan position, however, came from Thomas Cartwright, who responded to Whitgift's *Answere* (1572) to the *Admonition* with a *Replye* in 1573 and to Whitgift's Defense of the *Answere* (1574) with a *Second Replie* in 1575 and *The Rest of the Second Replie* in 1577. Cartwright was another of the younger reformers who had been an undergraduate at

Cambridge during its most radical period but had withdrawn from the University and begun the study of law
during Mary's regime. Upon the accession of Elizabeth he
had returned to Cambridge and become a fellow, and in
a public disputation before Elizabeth he took (with Thomas
Preston) the negative side of the proposition "Monarchy
is the best form of Government for a Republic." He became
Lady Margaret Professor of Divinity and a stirring critic
of the church, advocating the Presbyterian system so ef-
fectively that the heads of the colleges (including Whitgift,
who was master of Trinity where Cartwright held his fellowship) were determined to refuse him his D.D. and deprive him of his professorship. They succeeded, and he
went to Geneva to study the Presbyterian system first-
hand, lecturing upon theology in the Geneva Academy
and attending, by special permission, a meeting of the
Consistory before his return home. He appears to have
been back in England at about the time the first *Admonition*
appeared.

Cartwright's defenses of the *Admonition* provided the
most complete exposition of the Presbyterian church system that was to be known in sixteenth-century England,
but it was too radical for the times and not radical enough
for some of the later Puritans. He was advocating a national church which would be self-governing through congregational meetings and synodical representation and to
which civil authority would be subordinated by virtue of
the magistrates' membership in the church and subjection
to its discipline. It might work in such a small city state
as Geneva where such a powerful personality as Calvin
was a minister and where Beza became one before he undertook his even stricter rule. But it could not work or
even be seriously considered in England with Elizabeth
on the throne and Burghley as her chief counsellor. Though
powerfully supported by Edward Dering and other pop-

ular Puritan preachers, by London merchants and Cambridge scholars, by the Earl of Leicester and even secretly by the Queen's Council, Cartwright was forced to flee to the Continent in 1573 and continue his controversy from there. Dering was forbidden to preach, and Field and Wilcocks were kept in the prison to which they had been consigned as soon as the *Admonition* appeared.

Furthermore, Cartwright's proposed church was not the pure New Testament church that the most devout reformers desired. Although he professed to be advocating a church set up according to the Scriptures, some of his interpretations of the Scriptures were (as Whitgift, with more learning, was able and willing to point out) eccentric and arbitrary; and in his dependence upon the Scriptures he turned away from the course of the Reformation by placing too much emphasis upon the ruthless legalism of the Old Testament. His church would be a territorial church, including all citizens, rather than a gathered church of true believers. It might be purer than the Church of England in its "face" and form, but it would be no purer in its membership. This was the rock on which the later movement towards church puritanism was to split into two streams. Cartwright's proposal evaded the reality of the problem by assuming that church members could be forced into the appearance of purity by a severity of discipline which imposed the death penalty upon individuals who contemned its ordinances. No act of conformity ever passed in England was as severe as the one Cartwright's plan would have required.

While Cartwright was abroad and temporarily settled in Heidelberg he prepared for the press and wrote a preface for a Latin treatise on church government commonly known as *De Disciplina Ecclesiastica*, generally attributed to Walter Travers, a younger Cambridge scholar who had been harried out of his Trinity College fellowship by Whitgift and

who had lived in Geneva. This was a systematic exposition
of the Presbyterian system which placed less emphasis
upon the power of the congregation than Cartwright had
done and advocated a more complete separation of the
church from such civil activities as the maintenance of
prisons, punishment for heresy, the care of the poor, and
the probation of wills. Although Cartwright was not in
agreement with it in every detail, he made and published
an English translation of it later in the same year (1574)
under the title of *A Full and Plaine Declaration of Ecclesiastical
Discipline* which was smuggled into England to the in-
creased annoyance of the bishops.

But Presbyterianism, depending as it did upon legal establishment, made no progress in England. Fears that some
of the more radical Puritans were engaged in attempts at
her assassination led Elizabeth in the fall of 1573 to forbid
all preaching and to demand widespread subscription to
her order of 1571 that the Puritans accept the Thirty-nine
Articles, the Book of Common Prayer, and the surplice.
The hysteria was over by the following summer, however,
when a new and more serious threat from the Jesuits forced
the government to take an easier line with the Puritans;
and the selection of the reform-minded Edmund Grindal
to succeed Parker as Archbishop of Canterbury in 1576
made possible several years of informal experimentation
in church affairs within and without the establishment.

Grindal was seriously interested in correcting the genuine abuses of which the Puritans complained and immediately took steps to prevent the ordination of clergymen
who were incapable of preaching, the preferment of ignorant ministers already ordained, and the ordination of
ministers who had no prospective congregations. He also
abolished the Catholic customs of baptism by midwives
and forbidding marriages during Lent. He reformed the
ecclesiastical courts and encouraged the continued edu-

cation and training of a preaching ministry. Elizabeth was convinced that this last activity was a threat to her prerogative and ordered that the practice of "prophesying" be stopped. Grindal refused to transmit her orders and was indiscreet enough to suggest that she should be guided by her clergy in religious matters just as she was by her judges in matters of law. Elizabeth repeated her orders directly to the bishops and, in 1577, had Grindal confined to his house and his income sequestered for six months. But it was impossible to deprive the Archbishop of Canterbury without serious scandal, and he held office, without power, until his death in 1583.

In numerous communities, during the time of Grindal's authority and that of his substitute John Aylmer, the Bishop of London, local magistrates cooperated with the Puritan clergy and defied the bishops; and the bastard uncle of Lord Robert Rich "did so shake up" Aylmer in person, for threatening the lord's Puritan chaplain, that the bishop said he had never been so abused at any man's hands since he was born. The Puritan members of the Queen's Council continued to give secret encouragement to the violation of the orders the Council issued at her demand; and the Puritan effort to build a church within a church, a semi-Presbyterian organization within the Anglican establishment, went on until Grindal died and was formally succeeded by Thomas Whitgift.

Archbishop Whitgift, whose early Puritan inclinations had been thoroughly overcome by his controversy with Cartwright, was as determined an Anglican as the Queen could have chosen. He immediately challenged the Puritans with the tests of 1571, which required them to acknowledge the Queen's supremacy, accept the doctrine of the Thirty-nine Articles, and declare that the Prayer Book "containeth nothing in it contrary to the Word of God." The first two were readily met. The third was not. From

all parts of the country came protests against it which
suggest that by this time the Puritans had become a well-
organized group keeping in close touch with each other.
The Council tried to call Whitgift to account, but he stood
by the Queen's known—though never publicly declared—
wishes, and went to a much greater extreme by revising
the *ex officio* oath which Church authorities could admin-
ister by virtue of their office and so make suspected non-
conformists testify against themselves. The twenty-four
inquiries that Whitgift drew up to be made under the oath
were "so curiously penned" that Lord Burghley thought
"the Inquisitor of Spain use not so many questions to com-
prehend and to trap their preys," but Whitgift stood by
them until 1585 when a compromise, probably effected by
Sir Francis Walsingham, gave the Puritans a breathing spell.

But they were to make no further progress during Elizabeth's reign. Two developments particularly damaged the
Puritan cause. One was the increasing tendency of some
Puritans to become what they were originally accused of
being—Donatists or schismatics who preferred to separate
from the church rather than attempt to purify it. The same
tendency had appeared during the vestiarian controversy
when members of the secret congregations signed agree-
ments to forsake entirely the "traditioners" whose discipline was identified with that of the Antichrist. In the
seventies such groups reappeared, apparently with formal
church covenants, and in 1572 some kind of independent
organization was formed in Wandsworth that gave rise to
a later tradition that the first Presbyterian church in England was formed there. The best known movement toward complete separation, however, was led by Robert
Browne, a kinsman of Lord Burghley, who refused to accept a license to preach even though one was obtained for
him. With Robert Harrison he established a separatist congregation in Norwich and in 1582 took it to Middleburg in

the Low Countries and used the English press there to defend his "Reformation without tarrying for any." He did not remain a nonconformist, but his writings gave his name to the separatist movement as something more extreme than the one ordinarily called Puritan.

Although the Brownists were careful to avoid any connection with the Anabaptists (who were objects of particular horror because of John of Leyden and the events in Münster in 1534), they were considered dangerous to the state and three were hanged for sedition in 1583. Nevertheless their number continued to increase during the next ten years until Sir Walter Raleigh estimated their number, probably with a great deal of exaggeration, at twenty thousand. Since they were easily discovered by their conscientious refusal to have communion with the Church of England, parliament attempted to control them by punishing obstinate refusals to attend church services by banishment and by death to those who returned. Two of their leaders who were already in jail, Henry Barrow and John Greenwood, were hanged in order to expedite the bill, and it was passed in 1593. But the Middleburg exiles had already returned to Norwich where the congregation remained in existence—as did a number of others—throughout the last years of Elizabeth's reign.

The other development which harmed the Puritan cause, at least for a while, was the appearance of the Martin Marprelate tracts of 1588–89. These were the product of another controversy between Presbyterian and Anglican theorists which began in 1584 with the publication of a small anonymous volume entitled *A Brief and Plaine declaration concerning the desires of all those faithfull Ministers, that have or do seeke for the Discipline and reformation of the Church of Englande* but commonly referred to by its running title *A Learned Discourse of Ecclesiastical Governement*. It had actually been written by William Fulke before he aban-

doned the Puritan cause and had been preserved by John
Field for twelve years before it was published as a timely
attack upon clerical abuses that could be corrected by a
"household" form of church government. It was considered important enough to be answered at great length in
1587 by Dr. John Bridges in a 1400-page *Defense of the Government Established*, which in turn was answered more succinctly by Dudley Fenner's 1587 *Defense of the godlie Ministers*
and Walter Travers' *Defense of the Ecclesiastical Discipline* the
following year. Both of these replies were printed on the
Continent because religious publications were strictly cen-
sored in England, and the one active Puritan press, operated by Robert Waldegrave, was in fact seized in April,
1588.

Waldegrave, however, escaped with some of his type
and was soon employed in the dangerous but highly en-
tertaining game of belling the episcopal cats. His employer
was John Henry, supposedly on behalf of an unknown
Martin Marprelate, and the first tract was Martin's "An
Epistle to the Terrible Priests" which was issued in October.
In it he attacked the Bishops as "petty popes, and petty
usurping antichrists" and the "proud, popish, presump-
tuous, profane, paltry, pestilent and pernicious Prelates"
as usurpers of authority in the church and defended the
"Puritan" system of government set forth by Cartwright,
Fenner, and Travers. He was serious in his opinions but
maddeningly irreverent in his attitude, calling John Whitgift, the Archbishop of Canterbury, "John Cant," and John
Bridges "John Catercap, who had been a dunce since his
schooldays." He was particularly concerned with scan-
dalizing the name of "Dumb John of London," Bishop John
Aylmer, whom he accused of blasphemy, stealing cloth,
misappropriating timber, making his gate porter a minister, and bowling on the Sabbath. Aylmer considered all
the charges serious enough to be answered, and he also

sent his pursuivants searching through London and the surrounding countryside for the secret press.

The press was moved to another base of operations and published an "Epitome" or sequel to the "Epistle" in November, which continued the same subjects in the same style. Now the author was taunting the bishops whose men were "posting over the city and country for poor Martin," boasting of his popularity with "all estates (the Puritans only excepted)" and at court, and regretting that the Puritan preachers did not like him because of his jests. This was followed in March 1589 (after another removal of the press), by a broadside of "Mineral and Metaphysical School Points" and another tract, "Hay any Worke for the Cooper," which derived its title from a London street cry but was directed against Bishop Thomas Cooper whom Martin identified as the "T. C." who had attempted to answer him. By this time Waldegrave was ready to give up the dangerous activity of printing the tracts. His ambition from the beginning had been to print Cartwright's reply to the new Catholic (Reims) translation of the New Testament, later a part of the Douay Bible. The tracts were quite different from this serious work, and Waldegrave retired to the security and solemnity of Scotland and left the press to John Hodgkins.

After moving the press again, Hodgkins, under the direction of Henry and Job Throckmorton, brought out two additional tracts (supposedly by Martin Junior and Martin Senior, sons of "Martin the Great"). The second of these was probably the most infuriating of the lot, both in its satiric wit and in its serious attacks on the Archbishop of Canterbury and his "brethren." The press was finally moved to Manchester, where it was discovered and Hodgkins and his two assistants were arrested and eventually put to the rack. The final pamphlet was a "Protestatyon," put to-

gether by Henry and Throckmorton, expressing concern
for the printers and a continued defiance of the authorities.

Despite the undoubted popularity of the Marprelate Tracts
(which at one time, according to Martin Senior, had the
archbishop's pursuivants haunting the taverns for gossip
and searching the packs of all travellers to London) they
did the Puritan cause no good. Both the Queen and Thomas
Cartwright were severe in their strictures upon them—the
Queen because of their threat to the dignity of authority,
and Cartwright because of their threat to the dignity of
the ministry. They were answered in kind, but the literary
battle over church government (there could be no other
while Elizabeth was on the throne) was not to be won in
such a controversy.

CHAPTER THREE

The Release of the Word

I

Although Protestants may not have been altogether in agreement about the precise nature of "the Word" they were unanimously convinced that it should be made available to the people. The Scriptures needed to be retranslated from the improved texts made available by Erasmus and other humanistic scholars, and they had to be put into the vernacular for wider dissemination. Parts of them had to be read aloud, sung, and preached for the benefit of the unlettered and for the many others who were more susceptible to impressions through the ear than from the printed page. And their meaning had to be clarified by explication and put to practical use by application to daily life.

The impulse for translation was by no means new. Printed versions of the complete Scriptures in French, Italian, Bohemian, Dutch, and four Low German dialects existed before the Reformation; and between Anglo-Saxon times and the fourteenth century enough translators had worked on various parts to have probably produced (or so Thomas More and others believed) the equivalent of a whole Bible in English. But no printed English Bible existed in 1534 when the parliamentary bill was passed which separated the English from the Roman church and put "the law of

God" above the authority of the archbishops of Canterbury
and York without specifying where the law should be found.
The Church canons—except those contrary to the laws and
customs of the country or dangerous to the King's prerogative—were to be kept in effect until they were revised;
and one early historian of the Puritans suspected that they
were never revised because of a deep-seated English preference for judicial precedents over codified laws in matters
of this sort. There may have been a certain hesitancy about
accepting the authority of any word whose meaning was
not subject to revision.

One reason for the ambivalent attitude toward the Bible,
which existed all through the reign of Henry VIII, was that
biblical reading was closely associated with the reform
movement preceding the establishment of the English
church by more than a century and a half. John Wycliffe,
in addition to being a radical reformer, was responsible
for the first translation of the whole Bible into English and
had organized bands of "poor preachers" in plain gowns
to take the Word to the people. But the time was not ripe
for what Wycliffe wanted to accomplish. His Bible (completed in collaboration with Nicholas Hereford and John
Purvey) was not printed until it had become a historical
curiosity, although it was so often copied that some two
hundred manuscript transcriptions survive; and he himself was persecuted by the Bishops, by papal authority,
and by the state. He could hardly be held responsible for
the Peasants' Revolt in 1381, but he and his followers were
associated with it; and the uprising of his followers, fifteen
years after his death, was stamped out in 1399 with more
bloodshed than any in medieval England. It brought into
active being the statute under which heretics could be
burned alive, and the only old statutes against heretics
which were to be left unrepealed during the reign of Edward VI were those against the Lollards.

The parallels between Wycliffism and later Protestantism are so many and the laws against Lollardy so persistent that it seems impossible to disagree with those historians who say that the movement was never stamped out in England but remained underground until it could emerge and play its part in the Reformation. Nor is it possible to doubt that secret Bible readings—to which the many manuscripts of Wycliffe's translation bear witness—helped undermine the authority of the Church. Yet Wycliffe's Bible did not carry the full authority of the Word of God. It was a translation of the Vulgate, the official Roman Catholic version of the Scriptures, which might lead people to question the scriptural authority for many of the practices and teachings of the Church but could hardly be set up in absolute authority over the institution which produced and sponsored it.

The new stimulus to translation was the critical edition of the New Testament in Greek brought out by Desiderius Erasmus, professor of Greek and Divinity at Cambridge, in February 1516. Erasmus was heir to the humanistic learning of the Renaissance and a man of independent opinions who thought that St. Jerome "almost seems to have been afraid" to have given a correct version of the "Greek Truth" in the Vulgate and was convinced that his text "now stands as it was written by the Apostles." Other scholars agreed. Although his university refused to accept it officially, the Cambridge chancellor, John Fisher, later Bishop of Rochester, was enthusiastic; and so were Thomas More, John Colet, and Cuthbert Tunstall who later, as Bishop of London, was to make strenuous efforts to suppress an English translation of the same text.

This translation was made by William Tyndale and issued at Worms in the latter part of 1525 after having first been suppressed in Cologne. It was based upon Erasmus's edition of 1519 and instigated by Erasmus's own plea for translations into the vernacular. Tyndale had actually sought the patronage of Tunstall at the beginning of his project but had found the intellectual climate changed. For in the meantime Martin Luther had made his German translation of Scriptures, Henry VIII had announced himself Defender of the Faith against the Lutheran heresy, and the vernacular Bible had become a symbol of Reformation. Tyndale was turned away by the Bishop but found support among the London merchants and was sent abroad by them to carry out his project under circumstances that destined him to be one of the first English Protestant martyrs.

Tyndale's New Testament was the first printed version of the Word of God to circulate widely in English. When it appeared English customs officers were alerted against it, but it was smuggled in and denounced by Henry's loyal bishops, who ordered it burned and threatened with excommunication owners who failed to turn in their copies. From 1526 to 1528 (when the source of distribution was discovered) it was secretly sold in England, and many more copies were openly sold on the Continent where the English bishops attempted to buy up copies at the source in order to destroy them. The Antwerp printers, pleased with such a ready market, issued three increasingly corrupt editions before 1534, and Tyndale himself was able to obtain needed cash by selling a large number through an English merchant. A rival but less learned translator, George Joye (who had been issuing individual books of the Bible from various continental presses), brought out a fourth Antwerp edition in the summer of 1534 which corrected the errors of the Flemish printers but also made the text somewhat less protestant; and this forced Tyndale to publish his own revised text in the fall and another with additional revisions early in the following year.

During this time the demand for the Scriptures had become increasingly vocal. Henry VIII had, in fact, promised a new translation when he called in Tyndale's testament in 1530 but had been held up by the bishops who continued to cite people before the spiritual courts for teaching their children the Lord's Prayer in English. When the separation from Rome brought the reforming bishops and Lord Thomas Cromwell (soon to become the Earl of Essex) into power, however, the situation changed, and, in December 1534, the Canterbury Convention formally petitioned the crown for an English Bible. Miles Coverdale was already working on his version of the whole Bible, translated from other modern versions, which was published in Zurich in the fall of 1535; and although the injunction, prepared by Cromwell, to place a copy in every church was not issued by Henry, Coverdale's Bible was reprinted twice in 1537 and twice again during the reign of Edward. Yet the King's new articles of religion in 1536 ordered preachers to preach a belief in the whole Bible, and an injunction in the same year exhorted the people to teach their children the Lord's Prayer, the Creed, and the Ten Commandments in English. It had become time for a Bible to be produced in England, and the London printers produced one—as a matter of private speculation. It was licensed only after completion and was, at the request of Cranmer and Cromwell, issued with a royal warrant that all subjects could read it without control and with a royal injunction to set it up publicly in all churches of England.

This was the "Matthew" Bible, compiled by John Rogers under the pseudonym Thomas Matthew. The disguise was necessary because more than half the text was Tyndale's, and Tyndale's was a name which irritated the King because he had opposed the divorce proceedings and set himself apart from the English reformers. Henry had tried to have him kidnapped and brought to England and—though Cromwell had thought well of him—had done nothing to assist him in 1535–36 when he was imprisoned for heresy, strangled at the stake, and burned in Antwerp. Rogers had used Tyndale's New Testament, his translation of the first five books of the Old (which had been published in Marburg), and his manuscript continuation through the Chronicles, supplementing Tyndale's unfinished work with Coverdale's translation. Rogers himself had contributed only the short Prayer of Manasses in the Apocrypha, the Lutheran prefaces, and the marginal notes. The prefaces and notes were controversial—and so may have been Rogers, who had been a pastor at Wittenberg rather than a part of the English Reformation, and who was not to return to England until 1548. But the text was the best that could be found in English.

In 1539 two revisions were made—one by Richard Taverner, which introduced numerous verbal changes; and another under the direction of Thomas Cromwell, which was magnificently printed by Parisian workmen. The former had no great influence. The latter (without prefatory material or marginal notes) was the "Great" Bible which became the official Bible of the English church when a new edition appeared, with a preface by Archbishop Cranmer, in 1540. Eventually the licenses for the Coverdale and Matthew Bibles were withdrawn, and the Great Bible became the only official English version of the Word of God. Some 21,000 copies are supposed to have been printed by 1544, and other editions followed throughout Edward's reign and in the early years of Elizabeth's until it was superceded by the Bishop's Bible of 1568.

Widely distributed though the Great Bible was, however, it did not satisfy all the needs of Englishmen for the Scriptures in their own language. It was a heavy folio, too bulky and too expensive for reading at home; and the small duodecimo Bible published in 1540 was probably in short supply by the time the Marian exiles set off on their wanderings. In any event, the exiles seem to have been acutely aware of the need for a more useful text of the Scriptures, and the major enterprise of William Whittingham, after he arrived in Geneva from Frankfurt, was the production of a New Testament which appeared in 1557. It was printed in octavo and also as a small duodecimo, only $3^1/_2$ by $5^1/_4$ inches, fit for any traveller's pocket and occasional reading and characterized by other conveniences: clear Roman type (instead of the black letter used in all earlier English Bibles), chapters divided into numbered verses (derived from Robert Stephens's Greek Testament of 1551), and "profitable annotations of all harde places" with "a copious Table."

Whittingham set the pattern for the whole Bible, translated from the Greek and Hebrew, to which Miles Coverdale lent his experienced aid until he returned to England in 1559 and left its completion to Whittingham, Anthony Gilby, Thomas Sampson, and others. It appeared in a small quarto in 1560 (with a folio edition, in two parts, something over a year later) and was immediately popular in England. The Geneva Bible was carefully designed for what the Puritans liked to call "edification." In Roman type and with verse numbers, it had a summary of the contents at the beginning of each chapter (and summary of "arguments" for most of the books), subject heads at the top of each column, maps of the Holy Land and illustrations or diagrams of sacred Hebrew objects, and an alphabetical index of proper names (with explanations of their meaning, so that they might be appropriately used in naming children) and another of the "principall things" contained in the Scriptures. Its most distinctive characteristic, however, was its marginal notes. These were of three sorts, kept separate by the method of notation: references to parallel passages to be found elsewhere in the Bible, interpretations of the doctrine contained in many of the texts, and explications of obscure words and phrases. Such an elaborate system of cross reference and explication made the Geneva Bible extremely useful and contributed to its extraordinary popularity (at least 140 editions were to appear, in England and abroad, by 1644), but the notes were responsible for the objections raised against it and for the fact that it was never authorized for use in the English churches.

For the Geneva Bible was an aggressive book. The text of the Old Testament was an independent revision of that of the Great Bible with reference to the Hebrew original in the carefully collated text of Pagninus and with the help of that editor's interlinear Latin translation and of Latin translations made by such other good Hebraists as Sebastian Münster and Leo Jud. The New Testament was a revision of Whittingham's, which had been based upon Tyndale's latest text, and the whole was done with careful regard to the Protestant version of the Scriptures used in Geneva—the French Old Testament of Olivetan and the New Testament, with commentaries, by Calvin's close associate and eventual successor Theodore Beza. The Geneva editors and translators made a considerable display of their concern for the text. They printed the Apocrypha (those books found in Greek and Latin manuscripts but not in the Hebrew canon) in a separate section and italicized all words (including conjunctions and articles) they had added in order to improve the style of a purely literal translation; and, when a word or phrase from the original could not be exactly rendered in English, they approximated it and gave a marginal note on the problem. Because of their use of Pagninus and Münster, they were much more aware of rabinnical learning than their predecessors had been; and, because of their use of the Zwinglian Jud and the Calvinist Beza, they were further removed from Lutheran influences. Most readers who did not accept it as the absolute

Word of God, in fact, thought of the Geneva translation as a Calvinist Bible. But the notes were more responsible than the text for this reputation.

II

Translation of the Bible, however, was only a first step toward bringing the Word to the people, most of whom could not read or be trusted to interpret what they might read. Traditionally the role of the congregation had been to worship, and the English Reformation, unlike that of Germany and Switzerland, had not been brought about by great preachers who exhorted and instructed the people. Henry VIII was in fact so disturbed by the appearance of Continental doctrines in England that in July 1536, he forbade all preaching until Michaelmas when it could be subject to control by the new articles of religion that were being prepared under his personal direction. These made the "whole Bible" together with the Apostles, Nicene, and Athanasian creeds the basis of English faith but preserved the Roman sacraments and ceremonies; and the King's injunctions, issued after his excommunication, required only that the clergy should announce twice each quarter that the pope had no authority based on Scripture and commanded that children should be taught the creed, Lord's Prayer, and Ten Commandments in English. Henry was willing for a while to let the English Bible be placed in every church and be read by any subject, and in 1538 he ordered the clergy to preach faith and repentance as opposed to works and pilgrimages; yet he had John Lambert burned for preaching against the Real Presence, and in his Statute of Six Articles in 1539 he made all independent preaching dangerous.

With the accession of Edward in 1547 sermons became

more important. Bishops Latimer and Ridley were among the great preachers of the sixteenth century, and so were such returning exiles as Miles Coverdale, John Rogers, and especially John Hooper whose ability to attract large audiences kept him in a position of influence despite his cantankerous disposition. The clergy, however, were by no means all in favor of the Reformation or of its rapid pace under the new regime; and, in an explicit effort to prevent controversies in religion, preaching was again prohibited until a uniform order of church services could be drawn up. In the meantime a Book of Homilies had been composed under the direction of Archbishop Cranmer which could be read in the churches and provide uniform instruction to all congregations regardless of clerical differences in opinion and talents. It consisted of twelve sermons (each divided into two or three shorter parts) on what were considered the most essential points of Christian faith and behavior, and it began with an assertion that everything necessary for salvation could be drawn from the Scripture and ended with an exhortation against strife and contention in matters of religion.

The uniform order of service was completed as the first English Book of Common Prayer and authorized by an act of Parliament in January 1549, as having been prepared with "eye and respect to the most sincere and pure Christian religion taught by the Scripture" and "the uses of the Primitive Church." By a parliamentary Act of Uniformity it was made the only legal form of worship in England, as was the revised version, issued in 1552, which gave the Church of England the most extreme form of protestant worship it was ever to possess. Both books were entirely in English, and both included instructive lessons from the Old and New Testament. The revised version also introduced the Decalogue and a rubric (insisted upon by John Knox) stating that kneeling at communion was not an act of adoration. Both prayer books were declared by Parliament to be "agreeable to the Word of God, and the primitive Church," and the Forty-two Articles of Religion, adopted in the same year, included an assertion that the order of worship was in no point repugnant to the wholesome doctrine of the Scripture.

The Word was being made official before it became clear. For the Articles also asserted that it was unlawful for the Church to ordain anything contrary to God's written word, and the Book of Common Prayer ordained such things as wearing the surplice, making the sign of the cross in baptism, and kneeling for communion. These were clearly not authorized by the Scripture, but were they "contrary" to it? Such men as Hooper, Rogers, and Coverdale, who were accustomed to worship in the reformed churches of the Continent held that they were; and the fact that all members of the English church were forbidden, under pain of severe imprisonment, to attend any other form of worship troubled the consciences of these and other godly men and produced the first clear signs of the impulse later to be called "Puritan."

But they were not troubled for long. The second Edwardian prayer book was in effect for only eight months before Mary came to the throne and used her supremacy to turn the face of the English church toward Rome. The insistent reformers who did not stay for imprisonment or death fled to the Continent, some in disguise. Many took the English prayer book with them and were allowed to set up churches following their own newly established order of worship. Others were attracted to the French form or were required (as was the original congregation at Frankfurt) to adopt it. Although the French form provided for set prayers and differed in details as it was used by Pullain in Frankfurt and by Calvin in Strasbourg and Geneva, it differed radically from the English service in permitting a free choice of the Scripture to be read, requiring a sermon to expound it, making no provision for congregational responses, and restricting the musical part of the service to singing a metrical version of the Scriptures (either a psalm or the two tables of the Ten Commandments, separated by a collect) in a simple tune without parts.

If the manner of worship was to be determined entirely by the Word of God, the French form was much "purer" than the English because it consisted exclusively of the Scripture, its exposition and application, and of prayers inspired by the promises contained in it. To many Protestants, in fact, such a service actually was the Word in its most efficacious form—brought to life by the Holy Spirit acting upon a godly minister and upon the congregation. To Martin Luther, a schoolman by training and an inspired preacher by gifts, the spoken Word appears to have sometimes had more power than the Scripture; and Lutherans in general, while placing great stress upon preaching, were more tolerant of ceremonies and less inclined toward a biblical purity of worship than were other Protestants. Zwingli and Calvin, whose training was humanistic, were more devoted to the literal interpretation of the Scriptures, but even Calvin, the most legalistic of the Continental reformers, apparently believed that God could somehow connect himself with the preacher in an almost sacramental union to give the spoken word power and authority. Throughout the Continent, Protestantism was a preaching religion. The sermon rather than the sacrament was the high point of the church service; and the sermon, in its interpretation of the Bible and application of a scriptural message to daily life, was an indispensable means of bringing the Word of God home to the minds and hearts of the people.

The English exiles who hurried home at the news of Elizabeth's accession in November 1558 had been variously exposed to Continental Protestantism. Some, like those from northern Switzerland and the later group at Frankfurt, had been allowed to keep the "face of an English church" by following the English prayer book and preserving their separate communion. Others—especially those from Geneva—had adopted the purer order of service and had been in full communion with brethren who might speak in different languages but appeared in the same spirit before God. The Geneva group were the slowest to return. Their journey was longer, and the congregation as a whole delayed for a while in a vain effort to get the exiles to form a united front for Reformation when they got home. Others stayed to complete the translation of the Geneva Bible. John Knox, who had raged against the authority of women, was not allowed to enter Elizabeth's kingdom at all, but he brought the Geneva discipline to Scotland and in 1560 made it the basis for the northern reformation which was eventually to have so much influence upon the English.

When the exiles returned to find a queen who was Protestant by necessity but stubbornly unreformed by policy and disposition, they had to make a choice. Those who had been trying to preserve the face of an English church could easily choose to work within the establishment, created by a new Act of Supremacy in 1558, while attempting to continue the Reformation from positions of power—although some of them, such as Dr. Richard Cox, were obviously greedy for preferment. Others—most notably Miles Coverdale, ex-bishop and the translator of the Bible, and John Foxe, author of the Book of Martyrs—stuck by the Reformed principles and remained completely unprovided for in the English church, Coverdale preaching in poverty until the end of his long life. For Elizabeth, though willing to use the Word as a prop to the throne, was not willing to release it to become a staff of contention

among the people. Before the meeting of her first parliament she forbade preaching. Thomas Lever, who had been
influential enough to persuade her to change her title to
the "Supreme Governor" rather than the "Supreme Head"
of the Church, defied her and became a forerunner of the
itinerant "lecturers" who were to exercise so much power
during the Puritan period. But Elizabeth was never tolerant of unregulated opinion, particularly from the pulpit,
and would permit the release of the Word only when she
could exercise some control over what was to be released.

One such control was over the biblical lessons which
could be read in church, and this was incorporated into
the new Act of Uniformity passed by Parliament in April
1559, which provided for the "addition of certein lessons
to be vsed on every Sunday in the year" to the Book of
Common Prayer. The newly revised Book appeared with
these lessons (but also with the rather curious omission
of the Edwardian requirement that "the minister shall turn
him, as the people may best hear"), and Elizabeth took a
personal interest in seeing that these lessons were appropriate. Another control was the licensing of all preachers
and the requirement that they agree to wear the vestments
used in the early reign of Edward VI, both ordered in the
Royal injunctions of the summer of 1559. But within such
controls the dissemination of the Word was encouraged.
Every parish was required to provide a Bible within three
months and Erasmus's paraphrase of the Gospel in English
within twelve and to set them up in the churches for reading by individuals. And every parson under the degree
M.A. was required to buy for his own use a New Testament
in Latin and English, with paraphrases, within three months.
Furthermore every parson was required to preach upon
faith and upon Protestant as opposed to Catholic "works"
once a month, and every parson having the cure of souls
was required to preach "in person" at least once a quarter

or else read one of the homilies. The ministers were also enjoined to instruct children in the catechism, Lord's Prayer, creed, and Ten Commandments.

The pressure for the release of the Word, however, was not very great during the early years of Elizabeth's reign. For one reason, the Protestant reformers fully shared her desire for a stable and orderly government. She was their protection against Catholicism, the defender of their faith rather than that of the pope; and the Act of Uniformity, however offensive some of its provisions might have seemed to certain of the returning exiles, was directed against the clergy who had held office and achieved power under Mary. For another, the means for releasing the Word were not available. The effective preachers who returned home or came out of hiding were relatively few, and the clergy of the establishment were untrained in oratory and unaccustomed—if not antagonistic—to searching out the meaning of the Scriptures. Enough copies of the Great Bible apparently survived Mary (who was less active in book-burning than Henry had been) to satisfy the requirements of most of the churches, for no new edition was brought out until 1562. And there seems to have been little demand for bibles to be used at home. John Bodley was granted an exclusive license by the Queen to publish the Geneva Bible for a period of seven years but exercised it only to import copies of the New Testament (presumably for the clergy lacking the M.A. degree) and a folio complete bible in the spring of 1561. England needed instruction before it was ready for the Word.

One means of providing Sunday instruction for the people was that of adding to the Book of Homilies prepared during Edward's reign, and that was adopted in 1563 when *The Second Tome of Homilies* was issued, dealing with twenty new subjects, some of them divided into two or three parts. A new homily, in six parts, "Against Disobedience and Wilful Rebellion" was also added after the northern uprising of 1568–69. But set sermons did not represent the Protestant notion of the Word of God, and there was a difference of opinion about them among the leaders of the Anglican establishment. During the vestiarian controversy Archbishop Matthew Parker voided all preaching licenses issued before March 1, 1564, and seems to have considered most preachers disturbers of his peace with the Queen. But the Bishop of London, Edmund Grindal, was of a different mind. Unlike Parker, he had been in exile abroad and was an effective preacher himself, and early in the controversy he had annoyed his superior by collaborating with the Mayor of London in appointing men to preach at Paul's Cross who had been deprived by Parker. Grindal was well aware of the popularity of preaching among the citizens of London, from the learned members of the Inns of Court to the rabble who taunted him for the square cap he reluctantly wore, and he was disturbed by growth of sectarian groups within his own diocese. He wanted a preaching ministry within the church. But the troublesome problem was how to get it.

The problem troubled other bishops as well, and by 1571 most of them either permitted or encouraged the practice of prophesying—regular gatherings of the clergy, such as had been encouraged by Bishop Hooper and John à Lasco in Edwardian days, for the purpose of exercising their ability in public explication of biblical texts. The practice at Northampton, developed with the cooperation of Bishop Edmund Scambler of Peterborough and Norwich, was well systematized. There the local ministers formally subscribed to a confession of faith, signed their names in order, and gathered each Saturday at nine in the morning for two hours of public prophesying and one hour of private consultation. Following the order of their signatures, three spoke each morning. The major speaker, beginning and ending with prayer, was allowed forty-five minutes to explicate the text, confute any false interpretations of it that he might know of, and apply it to the comfort of his audience—all under the strict injunction that "he shall not digress, dilate, nor amplify that place of scripture whereof he treateth to any common place, further than the meaning of the said scripture." Each of the minor speakers was allowed fifteen minutes to supplement the remarks of the first, but without repetition and without "impugning the same, except any have spoken contrary to the scriptures." After the public exercises were brought to an end by the moderator the "learned brethren" were called together to judge the exposition and "propound their doubts or question," and the text for the next meeting was read and the names of the speakers publicly announced.

Such exercises, systematically conducted throughout England, could have trained a preaching ministry, but they would have required the unusual circumstances that prevailed at Northampton—the approval and active cooperation of the bishop, the mayor, and the Queen's justices of peace. But few bishops were as concerned as Scambler (who had risked his life as leader of one of the underground congregations in Mary's reign), and Elizabeth was determined to suppress the practice. The Word was in fact being curiously explicated by members of such sects as the Family of Love, the Family of the Mount, the Essentialists, and the reviving Anabaptists (two of whom were burnt in 1575): and the Queen was probably suspicious of any religious gatherings, unauthorized by the law, for scriptural discovery. She had ordered Archbishop Parker to suppress prophesying, only to have her orders quietly countermanded by her own Council; but she was insistent with his successor Grindal, with additional orders to reduce the number of preachers to three or four in each county. Grindal flatly and boldly refused. Defending preaching on scriptural authority and grounds of policy, he reminded the Queen that she was mortal and that a mightier prince "dwelleth in heaven"; and he offered to resign his see because he could not "with safe conscience and without the offense of the majesty of God" obey the Queen's commands.

Elizabeth stripped him of his authority without accepting his offer, but her own personal efforts failed to stop the practice. Even with the willing cooperation of John Aylmer, Bishop of London, who took over many of Grindal's duties, she could not find deputies capable of suppressing the now frankly Puritan lecturers who were being supported by wealthy laymen, municipal officials, and congregations who selected their own ministers and sometimes purchased the right to do so. Prophesying continued, often with the approval or active support of some bishops, although occasionally under some other name. Psalm-singing, encouraged by the publication of the Sternhold and Hopkins translation in the 1562 Prayer Book and in many copies of the Geneva Bible, also became a widespread practice. The sound was louder and more persistent in some districts than in others, and it rose and fell with changing circumstances; but for the last two decades of Elizabeth's reign the Word of God was to be audible in one form or another all over England.

Such interpretations of the Word were especially offensive to Richard Cox (who had been responsible for Whittingham's exile from Frankfurt to Geneva and who was now Bishop of Ely), and by January 19, 1561, he was suggesting to Archbishop Matthew Parker that the translation of the Bible "be committed to mete men" for viewing over and amending. Parker adopted the suggestion, drew up rules for revision (which included instructions "to make no bitter notis upon any text, or yet to set downe any determination in places of controversie"), and parceled it out to various bishops or bishops-to-be for correction with reference to the original Greek or Hebrew. Parker himself did more of the work than any other individual, writing the prefaces and preparing the texts of Genesis and Exodus, the first two Gospels, and, with the exception of I Corinthians, all of Paul's epistles (introducing surprisingly few variations from the Geneva text). The work was uneven, but it was completed and published in 1568, and in 1571 the Convocation of Anglican clergy required that it be read in all the churches. Thus it became the official version of the Word until it was superceded by the King James Bible in 1611.

This "Bishop's Bible," however, did not become popular for private reading. The Geneva or "Breeches" Bible continued to be published by the Queen's own printer and to be used publicly by some and privately by many ministers. More than any other version before that authorized by King James, it was a people's Bible—to be read at home, studied, and discussed by private individuals who were earnestly trying to discover whether they were on the right road to eternity. For them the cross references, the clarification of dark places, and the marginal annotations and interpretations were instructive and helpful; and many of the marginal notes, from long association, came to be absorbed into the "clear" or self-evident meaning of the text. King James was wise when he railed against some of them (such as the note on II Chronicles, xv, 16, which charged King Asa with lacking zeal for merely deposing rather than killing his mother) as "partiall, untrue, seditious, and savouring too much of dangerous and trayterous concepts," because time was to prove him right. The Word of God, as it came from Geneva, produced zealous followers.

III

The practice of prophesying resulted in sermons quite different in kind from those preached by Bishop Latimer and his contemporaries or those found in the Book of Homilies. These were instructive and exhortative on matters of belief and behavior, but their substance did not necessarily grow out of the Scriptures although biblical texts were regularly adduced to support their arguments. The method of the prophesyings, however, was based upon that of the great expository sermons of the Continental reformers who had systematically expounded the Scriptures in a way that extended their implications into every aspect of human life. The English Puritans were, in time, to produce their own expositions. But prophesying was designed to train inexperienced preachers, in a limited way, to explore the meaning of a biblical text in all its possible ramifications. The explication of the text came first, the application afterward. A skillful preacher might become expert in choosing his text for its applicability; but his training was in method. And his method was one of appearing to depend entirely upon the revealed Word.

What the earliest prophesiers actually did is not a matter of record. But what the later ones were supposed to do was set forth by one of the most influential of the Elizabethan Puritans, William Perkins, in *The Art of Prophecying*, which was "written in his younger years" (he was born in 1558), published in Latin in 1592, and translated into English by Thomas Tuke in 1606. Perkins based his treatise on the authority of the passage in Nehemiah in which Ezra the scribe stood upon a pulpit of wood, opened the book in the sight of the people, and blessed the Lord while they worshipped. Ezra and other scribes "read in the book of the Law of God distinctly, and gave the sense, and caused them to understand the reading." But Perkins was concerned with the whole Word of God and not merely with the Law. "The Word of God is the whole and onely matter, about which preaching is exercised," he wrote: "it is the field in which the Preacher must containe himselfe." "The Word of God is the wisdom of God concerning the truth, which is according unto godliness descending from above." It was "in the holy Scripture" because "the Scripture is the word of God in a language fit for the Church by men immediately called to be *Clerkes*, or *Secretaries* of the Holy Ghost." But he quite evidently believed that God was calling preaching ministers to make the Scriptures audible and edifying and was preparing his own treatise for the purpose of showing them how.

His authority for method was St. Paul, who had advised Timothy about "dividing the word of truth" by a process that Perkins interpreted as "right cutting" in two ways—resolution or partition, and application. Its resolution could also be undertaken in two ways—by "notation" or observing the doctrine clearly expressed in the text, and by "collection" which was necessary "when the doctrine not expressed is soundly gathered out of the text." To the editors of the Geneva Bible the "right" dividing of the "word of truth" consisted of "adding nothing to it, neither overstepping any thing, neither mangling it, nor renting it in sunder, nor wresting of it; but marking diligently what his hearers are able to heare, and what is fit to edifying." This agreed with what Perkins meant by "notation"—an emphasis upon the plain meaning of text which the Protestants adopted in opposition to the esoteric levels of meaning attributed to the Scriptures by Catholic commentators.

His emphasis upon a second method of textual explication by the "collection" or gathering of meanings was also covered by a rule: "In gathering of doctrines wee must specially remember, that an example in his own kinde, that is, an Ethicke, Oeconomicke, Politicke, Ordinaire, and

Extraordinaire example, hath the virtue of a generall rule in Ethike, Oeconomicke, Politicke, Ordinarie, and Extraordinarie matters," for St. Paul had said *whatsoever is written, is written for our learning.* "And it is a Principle in Logick," Perkins added, "that the *genus* is actually in all the *species:* and the rule in Opticks, that the general species of things are perceived before the particular." The method of "collection," in short, was a method of analysis based upon the assumption that every particular statement in the Bible represented "the wisdom of God concerning the truth" in some recognizable category and, as such, could be treated as a generality from which numerous other particulars could be derived by logical inference.

Perkins was probably remembering Thomas Wilson's *The Rule of Reason* (written in King Edward's day) when he spoke of the general being found in the species and may also have drawn his "rule in Opticks" from Wilson's observation that you recognized an approaching figure as a man before you identified him as an acquaintance. But when Perkins thought of the resolution of a text in terms of "partition" he adopted a system for dividing the Word which the makers of the Geneva Bible had not yet mastered. It was a system of analysis by dichotomizing which was to become common among the Puritans, and it is nowhere better illustrated during the Elizabethan period than in the works of Perkins's older and more famous contemporary, Thomas Cartwright. In discussing "the parts of God's word" in *A Treatise of Christian Religion,* for instance, Cartwright made them essentially two, the doctrine of the Covenant of Words ("called the Law") and that of the Covenant of Grace. The Law was either General (the moral law which came before the Gospel and was summarized in the two commandments of Christ: "Love the Lord thy God . . . and thy neighbor as thyself") or Special (the Ten Commandments given to Moses).

As the General Law was divided into two parts dealing with man's obligations to God and to his neighbor, so was the Special Law of the Commandments. Those of the First Table (one through four in the English Bible, though they would have been one through five in the Catholic and Lutheran arrangement) were concerned with God's worship, both inwardly (1) and outwardly (2–4); and those of the Second Table (five through ten) with man's duties toward his fellow man. These duties involved either behavior toward special persons (5: obedience) and toward mankind as a whole (6: murder, 7: adultery, 8: theft, and 9: false witness) or mere thoughts of evil (10: covetousness)—although those involving behavior could also be violated secretly in the mind. Within this analytic framework Cartwright was able to refine the implications of each commandment to such an extent that he could make the Law cover every aspect of human thought and behavior.

The Covenant of Grace was subjected to a similar analysis by being divided into two considerations, first, of Grace itself; and, second, of "the foundation thereof." Grace itself came in "parts" or "sorts." The two parts of Grace were God's agreement with man ("A free offer of salvation unto a sinner, upon this condition, that he will believe in Christ") and man's with God ("An acceptance of this offer by submitting to the condition"). The two sorts were set forth in the Old and in the New Testament. The foundation of Grace was "Christ Jesus." This also was subject to more analysis elsewhere, for the Covenant of Grace was considerably more complicated—or difficult to explain—than the Covenant of Works or the Law.

That so many Puritans should have adopted this pattern of thinking in dichotomies is perhaps explicable on several grounds. In the first place, the whole Reformation had been conducted on an uncompromising either-or basis. One's affiliation was with the church of the true Christ or

with that of the Anti-Christ. Salvation was either by Faith
or by Works. The authority of the Word was set against
the authority of the Church. Conscience was opposed to
dogma. Sin was absolute: there were no "venial" sins to
be mediated by man. The dead went immediately to hell
or to heaven: there was no indeterminate state of purgatory. Man's only effective act was, with the assistance of
God, to choose. Catholic dogma had been created by the
"if this—and that—then such" reasoning of the School-
men, and the Reformers were vehemently opposed to it.
It was not unnatural that in the intensity of their opposition
they should have turned to an "either this—or that" method
of searching out the truth. It was simpler. It lent itself to
the comprehension of the common man whom the Reformers were anxious to persuade. And it enabled such a
Cambridge teacher as William Perkins (as even Bishop
Thomas Fuller was willing to say) to humble "the towering
speculations of philosophers into practice and morality."

From a broader point of view, it was a way of thinking
that was appropriate to an age of exploration—exploration
which was as attractive to such a staunch Puritan as Sir
Francis Drake (who made his distinguished Spanish cap-
tives read regularly in Foxe's Book of Martyrs) as to the
suspected atheist Sir Walter Raleigh. But the Puritan
preachers or "teachers," as they preferred to call themselves, were less concerned with the exploration of the
globe than with the secrets of eternal life, and the Bible
was their unsailed sea. Products of the new humanistic
spirit of enthusiasm for textual study, they had before them
for the first time the true text of God's word—in the original languages used as many believed, for dictation by the
Holy Ghost—to translate and expound. The exploration
of its meaning was humanism directed toward godliness,
and "the calling of a Prophet or teacher," said William
Perkins, was "above all other."

The Puritans thought that this way of thinking was logical, and they called the systematic representation of it—to the great confusion of later generations—"logic." Perkins identified the system when he said that the interpretation of the Word should be "by the helpe of the nine arguments, that is, of the causes, effects, subjects, adjuncts, dissentanies, comparatives, names, distribution, and definition." This was a specific reference to the system devised by the French Protestant, Peter Ramus, and the first six arguments were an abbreviated version of the primary ways in which Ramus would have a subject considered while the last three were his representation of the ways which "grew out of the first." Perkins also reflected the Protestantism of Ramus (who made testimony a secondary and subordinate means of discovering the truth because it had no power of persuasion within itself) when he insisted that in preaching "human testimonies, whether of the Philosophers, or of the Fathers, are not to be alleadged."

Few preachers had occasion to use all the arguments in a single sermon or treatise, and few gave evidence of the number they used in discovering or "collecting" the doctrines they preached. For the Ramists made a distinction between the means they used in discovering the truth and the method they used in presenting it, and they also tended to keep the means secret. Perkins was explicit in saying that "In the *Promulgating* two things are required: the hiding of humane wisdom, and the demonstration (or shewing) of the spirit"—that is, art should be used in preparing sermons but should not be evident in the delivery of them. The best method of preaching was for the minister to feel the sentiment conveyed, for "wood capable of fire, doth not burne, unless fire be put to it: and he must first be godly affected himselfe, who would stirre up godly affections in other men." Even Thomas Cartwright presented

A Treatise of Christian Religion in the form of a cathechism that disguised the system of dividing the Word he used and plainly set it forth in a diagram at the beginning of each chapter.

Because sixteenth-century preachers of all sorts seem to have been more concerned with the seventh than any other commandment in the second table, their treatment of adultery may provide the best example of how the Puritans, by the use of Ramist method of partition or dividing, extended the authority of the Word into the realm of social behavior. The first Book of Homilies had contained three sermons on the subject ("that vice" which "at this day reigneth most above all other vices") based upon the seventh commandment and copiously supported by other biblical references. But their general heading was "Whoredom and Uncleanness" and they extended the strict meaning of adultery itself only to include "all unlawful use of those parts which be ordained for generation." Cartwright in contrast undertook to explore, by a systematic use of dichotomies, the meaning of the word so fully that for once his outline table did not provide room for all the distinctions he made in his text.

To the Puritan Cartwright adultery could be either "inward, of the heart," or "outward" with regard to the body, and the body could be abused in "things belonging" to it or in "itself." Among the things belonging to the body were external apparel (ranging from that appropriate to the opposite sex to that which was merely "new-fangled") and internally consumed meat and drink which might be sinful in quality ("too much daintiness," etc.) or quantity. The body itself could be abused either in its parts or adjuncts (tongue, eyes, ears, etc., by filthy talk or wanton glances and listening) or as a whole, either "by himself" ("as in idleness" as well as sexually) and "with others." Abuse with others was subdivided to consist of unlawful "con-

junction," which might be "natural" (as in either fornication or adultery) or "unnatural" with one's "own kind" or
with "other kind," or (as the opposite of "conjunction") in
unlawful "separation" which might exist when husband
and wife were together but "when due benevolence is not
yielded" or when they were separated by prolonged trav-
els, imprisonment, "mislike," or illegal separation imposed
by magistrates. To a Puritan who followed Cartwright's
system the indulgence in a choice bit of meat, a new bonnet
in the latest style, or the relaxation of a lazy day (or even
the thought of such things "of the heart") was against the
Word—and so might be a minister's longing for clerical
vestments and so were the separate establishments which
Elizabeth favored for her married bishops. That this particular Word should be the commandment against adultery—and that frigidity or fear should be considered a form
of adultery—is a tribute to the far-reaching powers of extension made possible by the subtleties of Ramist logic.

But the Puritans were able to go beyond the extensive
powers of their logic by an analogical collection of doctrines from the Scriptures. Although they usually objected
to the Catholic allegorization of the Bible, Perkins said with
reference to the collection of doctrines: "It shall be lawfull
also to gather Allegories: for they are arguments taken
from things that are like, and Paul in his teaching useth
them often, I. *Cor.* 9.9. But they are to be used with these
caveats: Let them be used sparingly and soberly. 2. Let
them not be farre fetcht, but fitting to the matter in hand.
3. They must be quickly dispatcht. 4. They are to bee used
for instruction of the life, and not to prove any point of
faith." In actual practice the skillful use of analogies was
a valuable technique in Puritan preaching. Speaking to
what Perkins called a "mixt" audience of believers and
unbelievers, ignorant and sophisticated hearers, a "teacher"
could make formal use of homely similes in order to clarify

his meaning at the most elementary level, or he might choose a text which had suggestive implications concerning political or other matters on which he could not preach openly.

However far the art of prophesying could extend the application of the Word, its extension by Perkins's precepts and Cartwright's example was not very great before their deaths at the end of Elizabeth's reign. Perkins's book existed only in a Latin edition until after his death, and Cartwright's *Treatise* was not published at all during his lifetime and was widely circulated only after his literary executors, John Dod and Arthur Hildersham, brought out a second edition in 1616 that was edited in accord with "some directions in the best and last copie that he left behind him" and with knowledge of the author's method. Perkins at least would probably have had it so, because his purpose was to teach rather than to disturb and he knew that he and his fellow teachers had to "hold a difference between *milke* and *strong meat,* which are the same indeed, but doe differ in the manner and fashion of delivering"—just as John Cotton, more than a generation later, held the difference when he dealt out "Spiritual Milk for Boston Babes in either England."

"*Milke,*" explained Perkins, "is a certaine brief, plaine and generall explication of the principles of the faith: as when a man doth teach that we must believe one God, and three persons, Father, Sonne, and Holy Ghost, and that wee must rely only on the Grace of God in Christ, and that wee ought to beleeve the remission of sinnes, and when we are taught that, we ought to repent, to abstaine from evill, and doe that which is good." On the other hand, "*Strong meat* is a speciall, copious, luculent, and cleare handling of the doctrine of faith: as when the condition of man before the fall, his fall, originall and actuall sinne, mans guiltinesse, free will, the mysteries of the Trinitie, the two natures of Christ, the imputation of righteousnesse, faith, grace, and the use of the Law, are delivered out of the word of God distinctly and exactly." Believing that "*milke* must be set before babes . . . that are rude or weake in knowledge" and "*strong meat* must be given to such as are of ripe years" and "better instructed," he could be primarily concerned with an "explication of the principles of faith" until the faithful were made ready for the subtleties of doctrine and "the use of the Law."

The translation of the Bible into English, the development of a preaching ministry, and the cultivation of the art of interpreting and explicating the Scriptures were all necessary for the release of the Word in all its power to affect the course of English history. But these were not sufficient while Elizabeth, whose attitude toward religious reform hardly changed during her entire reign, held firm sway over the country and kept Puritan preaching under some kind of constraint. During the latter part of her reign a substantial part of the populace came to be nourished by the spiritual milk of Puritanism, but how many were weaned of it and ready to rage for strong meat did not become evident until a new monarch ascended the throne and underestimated the appetite of his people.

PART TWO

The Puritans in Old and New England

CHAPTER FOUR

The Puritans
in Old and
New England

I

When I first thought of taking a new look at the Puritans of both Old and New England I already knew something about the complexities of their period and was fully aware of the proverb that "fools rush in where angels fear to tread." But I hoped that by dwelling for a while among the Saints on both sides of the Atlantic I might acquire wisdom. I have. Its essence may be put in the form of a new proverb: When the Saints come marching in, a wise man gets the hell out.

For the Saints—as King Charles I and so many others learned before me—were a troublesome people, unmanageable by the church and state, and also by the historian because of their tendencies to group and ungroup themselves in terms of political and ecclesiastical aims and sectarian doctrines. My only hope was to find some practical device for getting one aspect of the subject under historical control. Since my main interest was neither in the Puritan Revolution in England nor in the American Puritans in isolation, I hit upon the rather obvious method of looking up the books published by the Americans, collecting the names of the English writers who sponsored them by writing introductions, prefaces, and the like, and making a checklist of their writings in an effort to assemble a body of material which was sympathetically related and which would thus form a sort of intellectual raft on which I might float through a sea of revolutionary chaos.

The need for a new look was suggested to me by the apparently paradoxical fact that Independency in church government was a "liberal" movement in England, opposed to a conservative Presbyterianism and leading to the toleration of sectarian differences; whereas in America Independency was conservative from the beginning and became almost completely reactionary, leading to an active persecution of the sects and the enforcement of a death penalty against Quakers. An analogy with certain events in the recent World War was readily apparent: Like some of the European governments who moved to England during the Nazi invasion, the American "Puritans in exile" became more conservative as the English "Puritans of the resistance" became more radical. There were also obvious analogical explanations for the English radicalism in terms of the practical necessity of tolerating ideological differences in a movement directed against a common enemy, the military value of fanatics, etc. But it seemed to me that there might be some more positive and perhaps more significant force operating in America than had yet been identified and defined—something still to be discovered in the history and literature of early America which should not be brushed off by the observation of an interesting analogy.

And so, armed with a list of perhaps a thousand titles, I descended upon the British Museum and settled myself among the Thomason Tracts in order to look the situation over. Circumstances prevented me from being as well prepared as I should have been, from forming as substantial a raft as I would have preferred to ride upon; and, from time to time, I may have ridden too many odd logs in too many different directions. I must confess that when I looked

over my notes in an effort to verify my general drift for
this occasion I was a bit surprised and more than a bit
doubtful about the wisdom of attempting this premature
chart of my course. Yet, since I am supposed to lead a
discussion rather than give you the word, I am willing to
drift along in the hope that you will find the course suggestive as well as erratic.

II

One of the most ironic facts about the Puritan period
was the Saints' own frequent complaints that it was a "name-
blasting" age. In the 1640s, as now, the word "Puritan"
was a term of opprobrium—"a long-lived murderer," as
one reverend gentleman put it, used "to kill sound doctrine, holy life, sobriety, all that is good"—and so loosely
used that it signified orthodoxy to an Arminian, sobriety
to a drunkard, and a Protestant to a Papist. It was so
"poisonous," said another, that it was 'not contented to
gangrene Religion, Ecclesiastical and Civil policy" but
threatened "destruction to all morality" until "even hon-
esty, strictness, and civility itself must become disgrace-
ful." Yet it was so convenient a term that the Saints
themselves felt compelled to adopt it with a more specific
application, and during the period of the Long Parliament
it seems to have been conventional to identify Reformation
in England with Puritanism and to recognize three distinct
groups of Puritans—"Doctrinal and moral Puritans," "Ecclesiastical Puritans," and "State Puritans."

My concern, in terms of these contemporary distinctions, is with "Ecclesiastical Puritans" who were in the
process of becoming "State Puritans." For to the settlers
of New England and their English sympathizers the reform
of doctrine was an accomplished fact. They dwelt under

the Covenant of Grace as expounded by William Perkins and accepted the five points of Calvinism as determined by the Synod of Dort. An acceptance of the Covenant of Grace distinguished them from the Roman Catholics who were held to live under a Covenant of Works. The doctrine involved in this distinction was briefly this: In the beginning God had made a covenant with Adam enabling him to work out his own salvation by obedience to the law. But Adam had disobeyed and thereby condemned his seed to a heritage of total depravity. Mankind still lived under this covenant because the Law was an expression of the will of God, but good works no longer provided a means of salvation and the Roman heresy was to assume they did and thus make men blind to their only hope. This hope was found by the Puritans in the second covenant which God had made with Abraham and fulfilled in Christ. In it He offered by His own free Grace to redeem a select portion of mankind and justify their salvation by the vicarious atonement of Christ. The doctrine of the second Covenant had developed out of Calvinistic theology, and to the Puritans the systematized five points of Calvinism simply clarified man's position under the Covenant by offering a solid doctrine which could be opposed to the inadequate understanding of the Lutherans and the heresies of Arminius. Two of these points stressed the total depravity of mankind and the unconditional election of the chosen few, and the other three maintained that the atonement was indeed limited, that the offer of God's grace was irresistible, and that the selected Saints could not avoid persevering in their sanctity. The Lutheran error and the Arminian heresy, in short, lay in suggesting that men had any natural capacity for achieving grace or any freedom to refuse or accept it.

Now it is true that the Protestant movement as a whole was based upon the substitution of the authority of the

Scriptures for the authority of the Church and that the Puritans were firm believers in the progressive unfolding of the full meaning of the Word. For "Truth," as Thomas Hooker observed in this connection, "is the Daughter of time." It is also a matter of fact that the Puritans were committed to an exposition of theological beliefs in terms suitable to the understanding of plain people. But it is a mistake, I think, to find in their refinements of biblical interpretation and in their everyday figures of speech the substance of a theology essentially different from strict Calvinism. I have no wish on this occasion to pick a bone of contention with the author of "The Marrow of Puritan Divinity," but the fact is that I have observed in this particular group no evidence of serious deviation from the doctrines I have just surveyed, either by bargaining with the Lord for their salvation or by demanding it of Him in any legalistic way. On the contrary, Thomas Shepard in New England recognized the dangers of misunderstanding in times of controversy and, as a representative of the legalistic ministers engaged in condemning Anne Hutchinson, preached against the doctrines which have since been attributed to a "federal school of theology." "It is a great plot of Arminians," he said, "to make Christ a means only, to make man a first *Adam;* setting men to work for their living again; for they grant all Grace is lost, all comes from Christ, Christ gives all, and then when we have it use it well, thus you shall have life, else look for death: So 'tis a misery every soul is in." Shepard preached this sermon in June 1636 and repeated it in May 1640, and it was published for the benefit of an English public on the eve of the Restoration as a fine example of "the true middle way of the Gospel between the Legalist on the one hand, and the Antinomian (or loose Gospeller) on the other." Shepard's own comment upon such doctrines was: "Men will trade in small wares, rather than live on another's

Alms. Do you think the Lord takes it well to make him a Merchant for your ends? Oh no, never look to have communion with him in this way!"

Consequently it seems best to march with the Saints in the direction they themselves thought they were going—away from the controversies over doctrine, which distinguished the sectarians from the Puritans, and into the second stage of reformation which was that of ecclesiastical reform.

III

The earliest Puritans had of necessity attempted reform from within their individual churches and had concentrated their efforts upon such symbolic relics of Roman Catholicism as clerical vestments, set liturgies, and kneeling at the altar for communion. They had no opportunity to reform the government of churches established by law, but when they got such an opportunity—either by exile in Holland or New England or by revolution at home—they immediately took steps to free themselves from the control of an episcopal hierarchy by means of establishing independent churches abroad or by abolishing the hierarchy in England. On such matters as these they were united, and they were also united in their abhorrence of sectarian differences in doctrine which prevented one church from communing with another. They believed in the spiritual existence of one universal mystical church and were ambitious to make their visible churches as pure as any human organization could be made under divine guidance. They had many problems to face, and at least two serious ones were implicit in their reformed doctrine.

First, as Calvinists they were forced to realize that no visible church could be wholly pure in its membership—

that the mystery of God's grace would conceal hypocrites among the Saints. Thus they faced the solemn question of whether they should strive for an unattainable ideal or be as realistic as the Scots had been and accept into church fellowship the great body of unsanctified mankind. Second, as dwellers under the Co̶ nt of Grace they were New Testament Christians a̶ ̶ 'orgot the fact. God's religious and moral law- ̶ d in the two tables of the Ten Comma̶r ̶ ̶ ̶eople, wherever expressed; but ̶ ̶ ̶under the two dispensatio̶ ̶ ̶ be made between t̶ ̶ ' those that we̶ ̶ ̶t Jewish ̶ ̶ ̶atholic in its de- ̶ ̶e people. The New ̶ Christians had been a ̶ ̶ of believers who were con- ̶ ̶heir belief and voluntarily gathered ̶ ̶wship. The revealed Word, in fact, ̶ ̶stent nor altogether clear in its guidance ̶ ̶n of church government. The problem was ̶ people who genuinely revered the Bible could c̶ ̶pletely disregard the Old Testament and carry out a major reform entirely under the direction of the New.

The actual solution of these two closely related problems seems to have been dictated almost entirely by circumstances. The Puritans in exile were, by virtue of their voluntary departure from England, members of gathered churches; and those who were led into Holland, where they were tolerated by a government in which they could have no part, avoided any temptation to become State Puritans. A small group of them who returned home in time to take part in the Westminster Assembly of Divines recognized their unique position and used it as an ethical argument to support the reform of church government which they proposed: "We had no new Common-wealths to rear, to frame Church-government unto, whereof any one piece might stand in the others light, to cause the least variation by us from the Puritan pattern," they said; "We had no State ends or Political interests to comply with; no Kingdoms in our eye to subdue unto our mould."

Their opponents, however, refused to accept this argument. "You had new Common-wealths to rear; to frame your Church-government unto, when you first fell into these principles," replied Thomas Edwards; "namely, the new Common-wealth of *New-England* to frame your Church-government unto, where some of you were first bound in your thoughts and purposes (as you well know) and I shall make evident." The justice of Edward's attribution of a New England political influence upon the Dissenting Brethren of the Westminster Assembly is doubtful, but it is a matter of fact that Thomas Goodwin and his associates were the most active advocates of "the New-England Way" of church government during the revolutionary period and were largely responsible for the publication of those books, pamphlets, and letters in which the New England Way was transformed from a somewhat casual practice into a theory of government and a pattern of thought which seem to have had a lasting influence in America however ineffective the Way may have been in the England it was partially designed to influence.

IV

In order to follow the development of the New England Way we must step backward a decade and a half in time, from the outbursts of the Westminster Assembly in 1643 to the establishment of the first Puritan colony at Salem in 1628.

Salem was an experimental colony, organized in anticipation of the great migration two years later and made
up of more fishermen than Saints. Historians are still de-
bating the organization of its primitive church and the
influences under which it was formed—whether it owed
its peculiarities to the advice and example of nearby Plymouth or to the principles the settlers brought with them.
I doubt whether the question can ever be settled, and I
also doubt that it is of any serious historical importance.
The church was by the very nature of its existence in exile
a gathered church, and its purification from all ceremonies
was an example of the Puritans' normal reaction to freedom. A formal covenant of church fellowship and an ordination of the minister by the congregation may have
been practical means of preserving unity in the wilderness
and independence from bishops—means to which the settlers resorted under the influence of principles and precedent. But in any event the little church at Salem had
neither the position, the power, nor the personalities required to exercise much influence upon their strong-minded
proprietors who landed on the shores of Massachusetts
Bay in the summer of 1630.

The Saints of the Bay—perhaps two hundred of the
thousand souls who disembarked from eleven ships during the first summer of the great migration—came to America for what they called "freedom of ordinances," and their
primary concern was for ecclesiastical purity. Yet their
leaders were fully aware of the political power which had
been exercised against them in England and for safety's
sake brought with them the patent which provided for the
government of the colony by its proprietors. One of the
first acts of the government formed under its provisions—
taken a year before the first church building was con-
structed in Boston—was what we would now call an act
of unilateral revision which restricted the franchise to church

members. Thus, from 1631 until a new charter was issued after the Restoration, the Massachusetts Bay church was in control of the state, and State Puritanism in the new world took on the peculiar cast which most historians have agreed to call "theocracy."

Yet it seems to me that the term is a misleading one insomuch as it implies that the clergy possessed a political power which was actually kept from them. For the most distinctive—and, to the English and the Scots, the most disturbing—characteristic of the New England Way in church government was its insistence upon keeping the essential power of the church in the hands of the congregation. The congregation called and ordained its ministers—its pastor, teacher, and ruling elders—and dismissed them at will. The congregation approved or disapproved the admission of each new member and the removal of any member for any reason. The power of public admonition and of excommunication rested with the congregation rather than with the ruling elders who might be called upon to execute it. Since each congregation was independent of every other, the control of the colony (including the civil franchise) was vested in small groups of individuals who professed allegiance firmly to God, doubtfully to the king, and not at all to any kind of ecclesiastical officer. That any considerable community of either Saints or sinners could survive under such a system of apparently complete independency would seem a miracle.

That the Bay Colony did survive and flourish as a coherent community, however, is a fact of history which contains no record of miracles; and the secret of its survival, I believe, lies in two peculiarities of the Puritan movement which can be easily underestimated in our modern concern for the economic and other material aspects of history. The first of these is the fact that the Puritan times, as one contemporary observer pointed out, were "preaching times" in which congregations were preached into armies and the minister was "both the old Trumpet of the Law and the new drum of the Gospel." The preachers believed, as they would have chosen to put it, in the Sword of the Spirit; for they had achieved their own positions of influence through the power of persuasion, often in defiance of constituted authority, and those who led the migration to the New World had every reason to assume that they could maintain an influence in the colony by a purity of spiritual "gifts" which could not be reflected in political and ecclesiastic institutions.

The second fact is that many leaders of the Reformation had a faith so absolute that it cannot be exaggerated in the guiding power of the Scriptures which they believed were literally dictated by the Holy Ghost. In one of the most touchingly intimate of Puritan sermons, "A Childe of Light Walking in Darkness," Thomas Goodwin refers to men who, "being sometimes led by sense and reason whilst they walk in darkness, . . . are apt to interpret God's mind toward them rather by his works and dispensations, which they see and feel, then by his word, which they are to believe." Even the best of churchmen, wrote Thomas Hooker from America, "are all but men, and may err: their judgments are *not the rule,* but must be regulated. Their power is under Christ, only from him, and for him, wholly to be acted and ordered by the authority in his Word." "God doth not command such things as are contrary to his Law, his revealed will, or right reason," declared Samuel Bolton; "yet he commands such things as are contrary to corrupt reason, and above right reason, and therefore his commands are not to be scanned: it is our reason and the reason of reasons to obey because God hath commanded." And the final rule for "a right understanding of Scriptures" offered by Ralph Venning was: "If Scripture speak it, believe it, though Reason cannot find out the reason of it."

This widespread belief in the absolute supremacy of biblical law was the prevailing belief among the American Puritans who based their first attempts at the codification of civil law upon the judicials of Moses, and, as we shall see later, it provided the basis for their sincere denial of any affiliation with the independent sects of England and for their consistent advocacy of the New England Way as a "middle way" in church government between that of Presbyterianism and Independency.

But at the moment we must pause and observe that when the Westminster Assembly met in 1643 the major problem it faced, as Professor William Haller has so brilliantly demonstrated, was the problem of discipline. The English preachers were flaming with enthusiasm. The Scots brought with them the cold northern light of experience with discipline. The sects were of course not represented in a body chosen to institutionalize Puritan orthodoxy. Gradually the Scottish experience and Scottish logic cooled the enthusiasm and began to prevail in planning a national church which would substitute the authority of an assembly of presbyters for the authority of an episcopal hierarchy. Only a small group of "dissenting brethren" stood out consistently against Presbyterianism and advocated the Congregational or New England Way. They were name-blasted with charges of radicalism and irresponsibility—justly so in the minds of their accusers, for rumors were rife in England about dissension in the new world and no one then knew exactly how the Bay Puritans were handling the problem of discipline.

V

The most remarkable thing about the problem of discipline in the New England colony, as we look back over its history, seems to be that it was not at all anticipated. The earliest settlers, who had formed seven small communities of Saints by 1632, had control over their unregenerate servants and artisans and possessed a land patent which enabled them to discourage the immigration of the fanatics who were to stir up so much trouble in England. Their government was vested in the proprietors who met annually in a General Court to elect the governor, deputy governor, and assistants who served as magistrates and managers of the colony's or company's affairs. The function of the Court was poorly defined, but it was primarily concerned with allotting land and authorizing new churches until necessity forced it to identify itself as a kind of parliament with the power to levy assessments upon the towns. It became a representative body quite casually when the colony became so large as to make a composite town-meeting impracticable and suggest the convenience of choosing delegates, and for eight years the colony got along without any formal body of "positive laws."

Quite early the ministers decided that it was against the Word for them to serve in the capacity of magistrates, and a clear distinction grew up between the officers of the church and those of the commonwealth with the former holding an advisory relationship to the latter. The ministers began to meet at regular and frequent intervals for consultation among themselves, and they were, of course, always in close consultation with the magistrates who occupied special seats of honor in their churches. It was an informal government of conscientious men in which the clergy exercised power because they were the keepers of the conscience rather than because they had any civil or ecclesiastical authority. They derived their influence from the respect paid their divinely ordained office and from what was called their "gifts"—that is, their powers of persuasion and their skill in interpreting the Word—and serious disciplinary problems arose only when some of them developed consciences which refused to keep the peace.

The first of these was Roger Williams who arrived in America in February 1631 and refused to join the church in Boston on the grounds that its members maintained communication with the Church of England and supported the authority of the magistrates in enforcing the first table of the Ten Commandments—particularly the keeping of the Sabbath—which represented religious rather than moral law. He was called and ordained by the church at Salem, however, before the General Court could make known its objections to his ministry; but he remained there for only a short while before joining the Plymouth Colony. In the summer of 1633 he returned to Salem as the lay assistant to its pastor and set the colonial authorities in a dither by writing a treatise denying the legitimacy of their title to lands received under a royal grant, insulting the King, and charging blasphemy against anyone who referred to Europe as Christendom. He appeared penitently before the Court, affirmed his loyalty, and offered to have his treatise burned, and in 1634 was again ordained teacher by the Salem church despite the objections of the magistrates. In the autumn he began again teaching the opinions of which he had been repentent in the spring and in April 1635 was called before the Governor and Assistants and "very clearly confuted" according to the Governor. But he persisted in his opinions and expressed others which opposed the administration of oaths to unregenerate persons and raised objections to praying with them even though they might be members of one's own family.

In the eyes of the Bay colonists, who had consistently opposed separation from the Church of England in principle and whose own unity was a matter of necessity, Williams was becoming a Separate of the worst sort. He was separating religious observances entirely from community and family life. He was called again before the Court in July, charged, and required to give answer at the next meeting. In the meantime pressure was put upon the Salem church by the refusal of an expected grant of land, and Williams himself, in a fit of illness, confirmed the authorities' worst suspicions by writing a letter to his church protesting that he would not communicate with the churches of the Bay nor with his own church unless it also refused communion with them. At the October Court the Reverend Mr. Hooker was chosen to dispute with him but failed to "reduce him from any of his errors," and he was consequently sentenced to banishment for his "divers new and dangerous opinions against the authority of magistrates" and for defaming both the magistrates and the churches.

The second serious case of conscience in New England involved the great John Cotton who crossed the Atlantic in 1633 and to everybody's satisfaction and delight accepted a call to the office of teacher in the Boston church. I say "involved" because the case really centered about Mrs. Anne Hutchinson who followed him over in 1636 and undertook to interpret his sermons to members of the congregation, mostly women, who gathered regularly in groups of sixty or more in her own home. I should like to be particularly kind to Mrs. Hutchinson on this occasion because if it were not for her cousin John we would not have this library in which to gather. Winthrop described her as "a woman of ready wit and bold spirit," and she was to prove exceedingly troublesome because she quite obviously did not inherit that flexibility of conviction which seems to have descended in the paternal line of the Dryden family. She was in fact (and I am sorry to say so in these surroundings) stubbornly opinionated and almost unbelievably outspoken in a community which believed that the Lord had enjoined silence upon the female sex. Unlike

Roger Williams, who was simply an extremist, Mrs. Hutchinson was a heretic who held that the Holy Ghost dwelt within a justified person—that is, a Saint—in a state of personal union which gave him spiritual immortality and perhaps some quality of divinity in the flesh. She was also considered an antinomian because she held that saintly behavior was no evidence of saintliness of spirit and thus seemed to be standing out against those laws of God that the Puritans believed a Saint must perforce abide in. Her heresy was almost identical with that which Ralph Waldo Emerson was to preach two hundred years later in his Divinity School Address, and the colonial authorities were evidently afraid that it might lead to the same sort of practical command that Emerson expressed when he told the Harvard graduates to "Cast behind you all conformity and acquaint men at first hand with the deity." At any rate, she was sentenced to banishment in November 1637, several of her most active followers were disenfranchised, and a considerable number from Boston and five other towns were ordered to deliver up "such guns, pistols, swords, powder, shot, and match" as they should have in their possession and refrain from buying or borrowing any other arms until permitted by the Court. The order cited what had happened in Germany "in former times" and made it clear that John Wheelwright (Mrs. Hutchinson's brother-in-law and most loyal ministerial follower) would not become another John of Leyden nor Boston another Münster.

The whole story is of a fascinating episode in New England history, but I am concerned here with its later effects, and these grew out of the behavior of the Reverend John Cotton. For Cotton, like Williams, had brought with him across the Atlantic a sensitive and somewhat impolitic conscience which he had revealed on public occasions although without any evident desire to create dissent or cause trouble. Mrs. Hutchinson had admired his soul-filling preaching in England, joined his church in America, praised him as the only minister in the Bay who preached the true Covenant of Grace, and professed to infer her doctrines from his sermons. In the early stages of the controversy he stood by her, in opposition to his own pastor and the influential John Winthrop, as an old friend in whom he saw no harm. When matters reached such a state, however, that a formal list of eighty-two "erroneous opinions" was drawn up and the first synod in America was convened to consider them, Cotton had reason to take counsel. After the errors had been condemned, the points of difference between Cotton and the assembled elders were drawn up, reduced in number, and carefully reworded until the entire body were in agreement with the exception of the Reverend John Wheelwright and several lay members from Boston who had already left the assembly. Cotton has been accused of cowardice, hypocrisy, political ambition, and all sorts of other things because of his behavior on this occasion and his participation in the admonition and excommunication of Mrs. Hutchinson afterward; and although I believe that the accusations were unjust I do not want the question of their justice to obscure the effective difference between his case and that of Roger Williams: Cotton submitted his conscience to external discipline and accepted the results. Williams did not.

Now, according to our modern notions, John Cotton's resignation and aboutface is rather scandalous and Williams is the man we are inclined to admire. And it is this that brings me to the crux of what I have to say: We cannot understand the New England Way of church government or the beginning of certain basic differences between American and English patterns of thought until we try to understand what was contained in the Puritan concept of "conscience."

VI

The word "conscience" is a crucial one in Puritan literature because in it were mingled, almost inextricably, two
conflicting lines of thought which were the source of infinite confusion. One might be roughly designated Platonic, and the other, even more roughly, realistic. The
Platonic concept of conscience may be found in William
Perkins who defined it as "a natural power, faculty, or
created quality, from which knowledge and judgment proceed as effects." Milton's conception of the "umpire conscience," planted in Adam, belongs in this category, and
so does the eighteenth-century conception of an innate
"moral sense" which is usually identified with "conscience" in most modern definitions of the word. As an intimate private faculty it could be searched from within by
introspection but was not subject to conviction from without by persuasion or authority. The Puritans were able to
reconcile it with Calvinistic theology by making a distinction between the natural or sinful and the regenerate conscience, and it is easy to see, I believe, how the introduction
of a supernatural quality into the concept could have led
to its deification as "the Christ within" or the "inner light"
of the Quakers. Roger Williams's outspoken allegiance to
this concept of conscience probably explains why he became so sympathetic to the Quakers in his own times and
why he has received so much sympathy from our own.

But the Puritans with whom I have been concerned did
not use the word "conscience" in any such sense as this.
As Calvinists they had no belief in the absolute goodness
of any natural faculty, and as realists they were able to
observe no marked improvement in their intellectual processes as a result of regeneration. Positive evidence on this
matter of course is rare—although there is an abundance
of negative evidence—and so I find another of Thomas

Goodwin's introspective sermons of unusual psychological interest. Preaching as a regenerate man on "The Vanity of Thoughts," he assumed on faith that "In *Adam* and Christ no thought was misplaced, but though they were as *many* as the *Stars*, yet they walked in their *courses* and kept their ranks." Looking realistically within himself, however, he found a different condition: "But ours, as Meteors, dance up and down in us. And this *disorder* is a *vanity* and a *sin*, be the thought materially never so good." Although there was said to be no other "heart so well headed, nor such a head better hearted amongst the sons of men" in his generation, Goodwin himself was not inclined to depend upon any spontaneous combination of head and heart; for "our thoughts, at best," he said again, "are as wanton Spaniels, who though indeed they go with and accompany their Master and come to their journey's end with him in the end, yet do run after every Bird and wildly pursue every flock of sheep they see." "This foolishness," he continued,

> is also seen in that *Independence* in our thoughts, they hanging oft together as ropes of sand; this we see more evidently in dreams: And not only then, but when awake also, and *that*, when we would set ourselves to be most serious, how do our thoughts jangle and ring backward? and as wanton Boys, when they take pens in their hands, scribble broken words that have no dependence. Thus do our thoughts: and if you would but look over the copies thereof, which you write continually, you would find as much nonsense in your thoughts as you find in mad men's speeches. This madness and distemper is in the mind since the fall (though it appears not in our words, because we are wiser) that if notes were taken of our thoughts, we would find thoughts so vagrant that we know not how they come in, nor whence they came, nor whither they would.

Goodwin's first remedy against the vanity of thoughts was "to get the heart furnished and enriched with a good stock of sanctified and heavenly knowledge in spiritual and heavenly truths"; and I have quoted at length from his description of the raw material on which these truths worked because I think his sermon provides the best available basis for approaching what I have called the more realistic conception of "conscience." The clearest approach to this conception I have found among the English Puritans is in a sermon by the Reverend John Jackson preached at the Spittle before the Lord Mayor of London on Easter Tuesday 1642 and entitled "The Book of Conscience Opened and Read." In it he asserted "that *Conscience* is not a peculiar and distinct faculty of the soul, as understanding, will and memory, etc., are, but the *soul reflecting and recoiling upon itself*." "It hath been long said," he admitted in a consideration of the difficulty of his subject, that "Conscience is a *thousand witnesses*; and it's as truly said, Conscience has a thousand definitions and descriptions." But "whosoever understands . . . these three English words, a *Law*, a *Witness*, a *Judge*, is in a good way of proficiency to understand the nature and essence of Conscience; for in the execution of these three acts Conscience officiateth and dispatches its whole duty." "Conscience is a *Law* propounding the rule to walk by, a *Witness* to give evidence for matter of fact, and a *Judge* to give sentence according to the evidence."

Jackson tried to absorb the Perkinsonian definition of conscience into his own by admitting that Grace and regeneration could imprint a divine quality of goodness upon the natural conscience, but he was emphatic in his insistence that a good conscience was directed by rule: "let a man acquaint himself thoroughly with that which must be the rule and law of conscience; for it is no matter how strong and active conscience may be if it be not first right informed." Then, "the stronger the better, or otherwise the stronger the worse." As the laws by which conscience could be informed he listed four: (1) *"Divine* law, which is the will of God revealed in Scripture"; (2) "The Law of Nature" or "that natural light and engraffed instinct written in our hearts," which was "a good rule"; (3) "The Law of Nations," which was "likewise binding"; and (4) *"Positive* laws," ecclesiastical or civil, which merely had *"adnate* rather than *connate* power." Granted the rule of Law and the primacy of the revealed Word, "the good eyes and lusty limbs of Conscience" were of great value to the Lord, for "a law without sufficient force to execute it is but a dead letter"— although "force without law is but a riot."

With this background of theoretical discussion we can turn, perhaps with some better understanding, to the notorious controversy between Roger Williams and John Cotton over "the bloody tenent of persecution for conscience's sake"—a controversy which broke out after the calling of the Westminster Assembly of Divines and was strongly influenced by the contemporary situation in England and by the experiences of both men with being called to account for their opinions in New England. The controversy was too long—especially in the details of its charges and countercharges and its relationship to the facts on record— to be reviewed here, and I want to make only two observations upon it. The first is that, as I have already noted, Williams stood on the somewhat Platonic definition of conscience which has prevailed into modern times and thus took a position which is readily comprehensible today. The second is that Cotton stood upon an entirely different definition and thus took a position which I believe is the more significant to our purpose here. For the phrase that John Cotton used over and over again in his defense was that of "conscience rightly informed"—informed, that is, by the Word of God rightly interpreted by the best gifts granted to a community of Saints rather than by the meteoric flash of an individual's own vagrant thoughts. Its significance lies in the fact that it was not a specious evasion of the issue, as many modern readers are inclined to assume, but an expression of fundamental princple which involved a whole theory of government and discipline in church and state.

"We approve no persecution for conscience," Cotton declared in one of his many efforts to summarize the New England position, "neither conscience rightly informed (for that we account the persecution of Christ) nor conscience misinformed with error: unless the error be pernicious, and unless the conscience be convinced of the error and perniciousness thereof so that it may appear the erroneous party suffereth not for his conscience but for his sinning against his conscience." The necessary conviction was not trusted to the vanity of an individual's private thoughts but to the expressable wisdom of judicious experts—the holy members of one's church, or a synod of elders—and was made apparent by formal admonition "once or twice" as the Scriptures had commanded. "Reforming persons," as William Bridge was to observe in England, had to be "self-denying persons": "They must deny their own wits, understandings, reasonings, though they be never so plausible." For the good conscience was one which could bring spaniel thoughts to heel and make them follow a master who was guided to his journey's end by an authoritative interpretation of the divine Word.

The New England effort to achieve discipline within the Congregational Way of church government, in short, had produced what we might now call a theory of judicial review of the individual conscience under the written authority of the Scriptures. This was the essential—but, as a theory of government, still undefined—characteristic of the New England Way between the legislative authority of assemblies which was characteristic of Presbyterianism and the lack of all authority characteristic of sectarian Independency. And it was the famed Middle Way which the New Englanders and their English sympathizers tried to urge upon an uncomprehending mother country throughout the entire period of the Long Parliament and the Commonwealth.

VII

Had the New Englanders been genuine State Puritans—that is, shrewd and calculating politicians—they would not have expected comprehension from the mother country. For the New England Way assumed the existence of a weak state which would be the instrument of a restricted church—a situation which would lead inevitably to a theocracy unless God's grace exceeded the munificence of a land which was attracting more settlers for economic than for religious reasons. England, throughout the reign of the Tudors, had been a strong state in which the church was a national institution and an instrument of political policy. The New England Way assumed that orthodoxy could be maintained by persuasion and the removal of stubborn dissenters from the body politic. The body politic of England was made up of religious dissenters who had passed beyond the power of persuasion and were already engaged in a mortal struggle for power. The New England Way was based upon a belief in the constitutional authority of the written word, as dictated by the Holy Ghost and interpreted by skilled divines. England believed in the authority of principle, precedent, and political power. The importance of this last distinction was recognized by the dissenting brethren of the Westminster Assembly if not by the New Englanders themselves, for it served as the basis for the dissenters' refusal to bring the New England Way up for formal consideration: since the Assembly had failed to follow Parliament's instructions to seek guidance solely from the Word, they complained, they had no acceptable grounds for the proposals they might submit.

So, England went on its own traditional, experimental way of trial and error, through Presbyterianism and unrestrained Independency and into the restoration of a more tolerable version of the status quo. New England undertook to set an example of Independent self-discipline while its English sympathizers resurrected old letters and published new pamphlets from across the Atlantic and supported them with letters and pamphlets of their own. Despite their steadfast opposition to Presbyterianism, the American Puritans began to find synods both acceptable and useful; and matters of doctrine were entrusted to their care while the spirit of Independency was preserved in church government—formalized, for the first time, in the Cambridge Platform of 1648 which accepted the Westminster Confession of Faith as standard doctrine and offered in return a standard model of Congregational polity. The Ministers and Ruling Elders of the church, put on the defensive by charges of escapism that came from troubled England and genuinely worried by the strife they saw there, became increasingly ruthless in their advice to the Magistrates until immigrating Baptists were whipped on shipboard before they had a chance to disturb the public peace and persistent Quakers were sentenced and put to death. The purity of the church itself was compromised in the Half-Way Covenant of 1662 which provided that baptism was enough to admit members "half-way" into the church and thereby enable them to exercise the civil franchise. Expediency and an aggressive State Puritanism, in short, were taking over the New England reformation; and the guiding principle of the Middle Way was lost sight of before it was ever fully recognized.

VIII

In a fashion, I feel by now that I have drifted far enough to have approached the Enchanted Isles—to have come within sight of something which may be real and may be illusion. Yet I am willing to drop anchor, at the risk of being out of my depth, because I have found that as a scholar I have become less interested in conclusions that can be proved beyond cavil than in more tenuous ones which suggest significant forms and relationships for matters of fact. For at times (as when looking over the latest bibliography of the Modern Language Association) I think that we literary scholars are mostly engaged in piling up busy work which is likely to topple over by its own weight and smother us and perhaps literature itself. We are like the seventeenth-century Saints, doctrinal, academic, and political Puritans engaged in quibbling and quarrelling as we waste the talents and resources that might be especially appropriate to the discovery of more vital matters—those subtle and almost intangible patterns of thought which give a different character to similar ideas and objects of interest as they are found in different civilizations and in different cultural contexts.

So I trust I may be forgiven for suggesting that what I see or think I see in the literature of these early Puritans is a divergence in thought which was to develop into the basic difference between the English and American conception of government as it was gradually taken over by the people and institutionalized in the world's two most stable democratic forms. The English institution is that of authority centered in a legislative assembly controlled only by the unwritten constitutional restraints of principle, precedence, and political prudence. That of the United States is one of a legislative assembly subject to the control of the written word of a constitution judiciously interpreted by a body which has no legislative or magisterial power but which has assumed the supreme power of persuasive authority. Some of the terms I used to describe the early New England system have, I believe, prepared the way for a suggestion of its resemblance to a later political system and have perhaps made the analogy clear.

Because the guiding principle of the New England system was never clearly defined by the men who actually followed it, I am not prepared to suggest that any clear line of descent may be traced from the half-formed ideas of the Puritan fathers to the more fully developed ones held by the founding fathers of the Republic or by the Chief Justice who actually reasoned our Supreme Court into the position of authority once held by the chief ministers of Massachusetts Bay. Nor am I prepared to say whether the most significant activity of a historian should be an investigation of the development of an idea or the investigation of a people's growing willingness to accept it. I can only say, with any degree of certainty, that somewhere and at some time the English and the American way of thinking about discipline and government separated—and that the best place to begin the search for the beginnings of this separation is, perhaps, at the beginning.

PART THREE

Renaissance Uses
of Ramean Logic

CHAPTER FIVE

In Solitary Meditations
and Deliberations
with a Man's Self:
The Logic
of Hamlet's Soliloquies*

I

For a good many years I have been interested in literature not only for its own sake but as a medium of inquiry into the history of the human mind. The patterns of what is sometimes called "intellectual history" are many, and one of the most subtle and interesting, to me, is that of logic. It is also a somewhat dangerous one to pursue because men seem much more tolerant of other people's ideas and beliefs than they are of different reasoning processes. "My reason is my friend, yours is a cheat" comes nearer being a universal sentiment than anything that came from the Earl of Rochester's pen.

---

*Privately printed and issued as a pamphlet in Copenhagen in 1964.
If I were writing this today I would be less apologetic and defensive about my departure from the Romantic conception of Shakespeare's creative processes. The new researches of Gerald Bentley on the professionalism of the Jacobean dramatists and those of William Ringler on the calculation required for the adaptation of Shakespeare's plays to the limited resources of an acting company have emphasized the craftsmanship of a dramatist who (I am now ready to believe) turned to a library for guidance when he wanted to portray Portia's legal reasoning and returned to it for *Hamlet* when he wanted to portray a man whose tragic flaw was not necessarily in his reasoning too precisely about an event but in the misguided precision of his reasoning.

At no time has this been truer than during the Renaissance when the new system of Peter Ramus came in conflict with Aristotelian Scholasticism in France and England. Abraham Fraunce knew what to expect when he adopted the Ramean system for *The Lawiers Logike* he published in London in 1588. "But loe," he said in his Preface addressed to the learned lawyers of England:

> I see on a sodayne this extravagant discourse abruptly cut off by the importunate exclamations of a raging and firey-faced Aristotelean; who seeing Ramus his Logike in some estimation, maketh small accoumpt of his owne credite in uttering such impatient Speaches.
>
> Good God, what a world is this? What an age doe wee now lyve in? A Sophister in times past was a tytle of credite and a woorde of commendation; nowe what more odious? Aristotle then the father of Philosophy; now who lesse favoured? Ramus rules abroade, Ramus at home, and who but Ramus? Antiquity is nothing but Dunsicality, and our forefathers inventions unprofitable trumpery. Newfangled, youngheaded, harebrayne boyes will needs bee Masters that never were Scholars, prate of methods, who never knew order; rayle against Aristotle as sone as they are crept out of the shell. Hereby it comes to passe that every cobler can cogge a Syllogisme, every Carter crake of Propositions. Hereby is Logike prophaned, and lyeth prostitute, removed out of her Sanctuary, robbed of her honour, left of her lovers, ravyshed of Strangers, and made common to all, which before was proper to Schoolmen, and only consecrated to Philosophers.
>
> I have heard the lyke speaches to these before this, and I look for no better hereafter.

Fraunce would not have revised his prophecy had he been able to look centuries into the future. Ramus, of course, had already had his library burned because of his opinions, and in twentieth-century America Norman E. Nelson has directed a scorching attack upon his memory and upon such scholars as Hardin Craig, Perry Miller, and Rosemond Tuve who have attempted to revive it. Yet the intensive scholarship of Walter J. Ong, the broad survey of *Logic and Rhetoric in England, 1500–1700* by W. S. Howell (to which I am particularly indebted in my introductory survey); and the yet unpublished study of Daniel Rogers (the friend of Spenser, Sidney, and Gabriel Harvey—and, like Hamlet, a student at Wittenberg) by James E. Phillips all bear circumstantial witness to the genuine and considerable influence of Ramus in his own time and in the century which followed, however reprehensible his influence may have been or even an acknowledgment of it might still be in the minds of what Abraham Fraunce called the "firey-faced" thinkers of other persuasions.

Consequently I trust that it will not be altogether intolerable of me to revive an old interest on this occasion and examine one of the most interesting Renaissance examples I have observed of the relationship of logic to literature.

II

The major problem involved in examining the relationship between logic and literature, especially during the English Renaissance, is that one must approach the subject under a rather severe discipline which is both historical and technical. The historical discipline is necessary because a certain pattern of thought may be "logical" to one generation—or to a group of individuals within a generation—and yet seem entirely illogical to another, so that any tendency toward absolutism in thinking or in the use of terms is likely to defeat the investigation at its outset. The technical discipline is necessary because the terms used for descriptive or expository purposes must necessarily be borrowed from technical treatises and used with strict reference to the meanings given in their source, however foreign these meanings may be to popular usage or however much they may differ from the meanings given the same terms in another logical system. Consequently the best approach to the logic of Hamlet's soliloquies may be through a review of the two logical systems that existed in Elizabethan England for the purpose of showing that the "logic" of the time was not logic in any absolute sense. Similarly the only accurate way to discuss it seems to be that of using technical terms borrowed from the relevant system or the possible source and to capitalize or put them in quotation marks as a constant reminder of their peculiar significance.

The oldest and most firmly established of these two system was the Scholastic which traced its origins proudly to Aristotle but actually included centuries of changes in Aristotelian theory. The newest was the Ramistic, a drastic and highly controversial revision of Aristotle, which had just begun to attract attention in England during the last quarter of the century. Both were disposed to break down Aristotle's distinction between logic and dialectic and make the two words interchangeable, and both divided logic into two parts—"Invention," an analytic process which was concerned with the discovery of arguments; and "Judgment," a synthesizing process which was concerned with the orderly arrangement or disposition of them. The word "Argument" itself was a technical one with different meanings within the two systems. The Scholastics used it in the sense, somewhat akin to its modern meaning, of "demonstrative proof." The Ramists (who sometimes substituted the word "reason" for it) used it to mean something which was either "self-evident" or at least affirmative. Such a difference in usage is emphasized by the fact that the Scholastics made the "Invention" of Arguments the second part of logic (on the theory perhaps that evidence should be found to support a demonstration) whereas the Ramists made "Invention" the first part on the theory that the discovery of truth should precede its exposition. Each provided formal guidance for the analytic process of "Invention," however, by means of a set series of topics designed to systematize logical investigations.

But within the framework of these resemblances the two systems were strikingly different. The topics of Scholastic "Invention" included the five predicables—which required a consideration of genus, species, difference, property, and accidence—and a varying number of others in a somewhat miscellaneous order. Those of the Ramists were severely limited to a series of primary relationships—cause and effect, subject and adjunct, differences in kind, and resemblances in quality and quantity—followed by a secondary list of topics "growing out of the first" which differed in form with different Ramists but usually referred to names, divisions, definitions, and authorities or testimonies. Individual logicians might subdivide these topics at will, but this highly systematized basic list was the identifying characteristic of the Ramean system. Definition obviously played a primary role in one system and a very insignificant one in the other, for the rival logicians approached a matter for contemplation with two quite different questions in mind. The Scholastics started off asking "What?" The Ramists, by asking "Why?"

Furthermore, there was a prevailing difference between the types of reasoning most commonly found in each. Since the Scholastics might have already set up a proposition in the first part of logic, they could and often did approach "Invention" with the two elements of the proposition in mind, run both through the list of topics, and test each possible relationship with a syllogism. The Ramists, seeking to discover a valid proposition, approached their topics with more openly inquisitive minds and simply examined a concept in the light of a systematic dichotomy of previously hypothesized relationships. The result was that the syllogism played a much greater and more apparent part in the Scholastic system than in the Ramistic while the latter depended more upon setting up alternatives or "dichotomies" and choosing between them. All the recognized types of reasoning, of course, were included in both systems; but there was such a marked difference between the two schools in their preference for the syllogistic or the selective process that the greatest and last of the English Ramists would eventually declare, in *Paradise Lost,* that "Reason is choice."

It was the frequent use of alternatives and choice in Hamlet's soliloquies which first suggested that the pattern of his meditations might be sought for in the jungle of Renaissance logic, in that part of logic which was called "Invention," and specifically in Ramistic invention. The suggestion was by no means a conclusive one, however, because rational choice is certainly not peculiar to Ramean logic, because the soliloquies are provocatively human rather than academic, and because logic itself is such an ingeniously empirical art that any single discourse might be analyzed according to almost any system. The problem was that of finding any formal logic available to Shakespeare at the time he wrote *Hamlet* which provided a complete pattern for all the soliloquies. The Scholastic logics offered no help at all unless one assumed that Hamlet avoided the Scholastic approach and its order of investigation—in fact, the basic framework of the system.

The most teasing of the Ramean logics was Abraham Fraunce's *The Lawiers Logike,* published in 1588, which was a particularly aggressive and impressive Ramean textbook. For Fraunce was actively conscious of the relationship between logic and contemporary English literature and emphasized it by drawing many of his illustrations from Spenser's *The Shepherd's Calendar.* Also, there seemed to be certain connecting links between Fraunce's book and Shakespeare's play. In the first place, *The Lawiers Logike* opened with a discussion of the question whether "logic" originally signified "reason" or "talk" and observed that "because reasoning may be without talking, as in solitary meditations and deliberations with a man's self, some hold the first derivation as most significant" (p. 1 rec.). Such an observation—taken in connection with a later insistence (p. 114 ver.) that the first part of logic was for the private discovery of the truth and the second part for the teaching of it to others—might well have recommended the propriety of using logical "Invention" as the pattern for such private meditations and deliberations with himself as Hamlet indulged in. Second, Fraunce was rather startling in his use (p. 86 ver.) of the phrase "to be, or not to be" as an example of an alternative difficult to judge because "not to be" might signify either death or life after death. There was a certain passing fascination, in fact, in speculating on the First Quarto stage direction for Hamlet's famous soliloquy which had him enter "pouring upon a book." Should he, perhaps, have closed *The Lawiers Logike* before allowing his mind to wander, as Lily B. Campbell has observed, through Cardan's *Comforte?*

But, actually, neither of these possible connecting links has more than an idle interest, for Fraunce's particular system does not fit the soliloquies. The obstacle is his treatment of the first and most important of the Ramean topics, "Cause." Fraunce follows the example of most Ramists by dichotomizing it into "Efficient" and "Material" on the one hand and "Formal" and "Final" on the other, and he subdivides the Efficient Cause almost as elaborately as Milton was to do later. Since Hamlet did not meditate at all upon final causes and made none of Fraunce's distinctions with respect to an efficient cause, he could not have been following this system either in its precise or in a simplified form. Shakespeare might have known *The Lawiers Logike*, and I like to fancy that he may have taken some suggestions from it, but he made no systematic use of it in *Hamlet*.

The only Ramean logic, apparently, that he could have used was Dudley Fenner's *The Arts of Logike and Rhetorike, plainlie set forth in the Englishe tongue* which had been published on the continent in 1584 and republished in 1588. For Fenner appears to have been unique among the early Ramists in that he disregarded "Final" causes completely and dichotomized the topic "Cause" as "External" on the one hand and "Internal" (subdivided into "Material" and "Formal") on the other. Since this was precisely Hamlet's procedure, Fenner's little book seems to be the proper one on which to exercise whatever "witcraft" is needed to grasp the basic principles of Ramean Invention and the procedure involved in putting it to actual use.

III

Actually, Fenner's *Logike* is not only one of the most distinctive but one of the simplest examples of the Ramean system. Like all others, it makes a careful distinction between the intellectual process involved in searching out the truth and that of expounding it and does so by dividing its subject into two parts under the conventional headings of "Invention" and "Judgment." Unlike the others, however, it does not divide the topics of Invention into two groups of "Arguments"—"Artificial Arguments" which were supposed to contain the power of conviction within themselves, and "Inartificial" ones, such as Testimony, which had only a contingent power of conviction. Instead, Fenner divided his otherwise unlabeled topics into groups of

"First Arguments" and of "Those growing out of the First," thus limiting the primary acts of logical exploration to a consideration of the standard relationships of cause and effect, subject and adjunct, differences, and resemblances. Divisions and definitions were placed together with testimony among the "Arguments growing out of the First" as distinctly subordinate topics for logical exploration. Consequently a person following Fenner could get at the self-evident logical truth of a matter much more simply than he could by following any other system. Fenner also appears to have simplified the mental processes required in the use of his logic by his tendency to substitute the word "Reason" for the technical term "Argument." Thus his system of Invention was a system of seeking the Reasons for something, and the most important Reason for anything was its Cause and the least important was Testimony concerning it.

The second, third, and fourth chapters of Fenner's little book were devoted to the primary topics of "Invention"; and the first chapter, although formally titled "Of a Cause," was actually devoted to what were called "Agreeable Arguments" which were subdivided into "More Agreeable" and "Less Agreeable" classifications. "Agreeable" Arguments or "Reasons" consisted of "Cause" and the "Thing Caused" or the Effect, and "Cause" itself was dichotomized into "External" causes which were "without the thing caused" and "Internal" Causes which were "within the thing caused" and might be either "Formal" in their reference to the essence or "Material" in their reference to the matter of the thing caused. As we have already observed, Fenner seems to have tacitly assumed that the "External" Cause was something like what most logicians called the "Efficient," and he did not concern himself at all with "Final" Causes.

This sort of description of Ramean logic can appear quite complicated, when, as a matter of fact, it is extraordinarily simple. Some logicians used—and Fenner evidently expected his readers to visualize—a table which clarified the dichotomy of "Arguments" or "Reasons" but was used only with reference to its terminal elements. In such a tabular form, Fenner's "Agreeable" Arguments would look something like this:

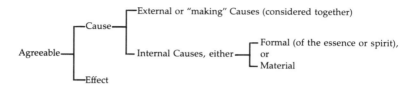

"Less Agreeable" Arguments consisted of those dealing with the relationship of a "Subject" and its "Adjuncts" and, in the form of a table, would appear as follows:

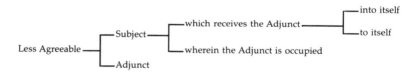

Anyone exhausting the logical applications of this chapter to a particular question would have to consider each of these four major "Arguments" and also each of the subdivisions as represented by the final word or phrase in each extension of the major Argument.

In his third chapter, "Of disagreeable arguments," Fenner made the conventional distinctions which may be tabulated without difficulty:

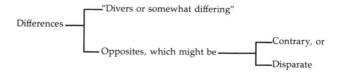

Chapter IV, "Of compared arguments," was almost as simple in its conventional distinctions:

To exhaust all the logic inherent in any matter, a person needed only to consider these four major "Arguments" and their subdivisons in addition to those surveyed in Chapter II. Other formal Arguments, discussed by Fenner in the fifth chapter of his treatise, were not inherent in the matter itself but were "more" or "less" artifical Arguments which required a certain amount of "Division" or "Definition" or else consisted of "Testimony" which might or might not enter into a case.

To a good Ramist, testimony was always of less value than an "Artificial" Argument which had the power of persuasion within itself by means of its self-evident truth. It could affect his judgment, of course, but he would have thought himself illogical if he accepted any testimony on its face value without verifying it with all the other evidence or Arguments his "Invention" could supply. Similarly, according to Fenner's version of the system, the amount of truth to be found in a "Division" or a "Definition" was of relatively small value. The trustworthy whole of the first part of logic was contained in the primary table of topics. Thus, an individual faced by a puzzling condition could get at the whole truth of his problem by referring it to the terminal words in the diagram given above. By their means he could explore it logically and discover the grounds for logical exposition or any other form of action.

It remains to be seen how they might conceivably have

been used by a young man who was represented as having just been called home from his university studies to find himself in a state of mind which suggested, first, that there was something wrong in Denmark; second, that something might be wrong with himself; and third, that his own mental state was simply incidental to some larger obligation he might be rationally expected to meet. Such a young man was Shakespeare's Hamlet whose efforts to come to grips with his problem, by solitary meditations and deliberations with himself, have a logical coherence which may be accidental but which may be curiously explained in terms of the system of "Invention" set forth by Dudley Fenner.

IV

There is no obscurity in relating the meditations of Hamlet in the first of his eight soliloquies (I, ii, 129–59) to the first item in this logical table. He is aware that he is suffering from a melancholy weariness with life, and, tacitly assuming that his condition is the "Effect" of some "Cause," he seeks the external reason for his state of mind. Almost automatically he dichotomizes his consideration of the world in terms of appearance or reality: either its uses "seem" weary, stale, flat, and unprofitable, or it is actually filled with rankness. But he hardly needs to pause over a choice. The rankness is real. His excellent father had died, and his mother, within a month, had incestuously married an unworthy successor. From this nothing could come to good. Such were the actual uses of the world, operating entirely outside himself, which formed the "making or efficient Cause" or "External" reason for his melancholy. The speech consists of a simple exploration of the first half of a single logical "Argument"; and Hamlet evidently thought it complete, for he brought it to an end with the conclusion "break my heart, for I must hold my tongue."

After he hears of his father's spirit in arms, however, Hamlet is not so sure of the completeness of his exploration. He suspects foul play, but at the time of his second very brief soliloquy (I, ii, 254–57) he is in no position to pursue his suspicions. Instead, he must make his soul sit still until his uncle's wickedness rises inevitably to sight. Even when his interview with the ghost directs his thoughts away from his own state of mind toward the fate of his father and the villainy of his uncle, Hamlet is in an ambiguous logical position. His conviction that foul play is a part of the rankness of the world is positive. But it is not rational. For it is based upon testimony, and testimony is an "Inartificial Argument" without the logical power of persuasion within itself. Yet the new, if unconfirmed, element of external "Cause" is capable of having a new effect on Hamlet's state of mind; and in his third soliloquy (I, v, 92–112) he reveals it in a transformation from melancholy to cynicism as he reverses the conclusion of his first soliloquy and holds his heart while his tongue breaks forth in a passionate expression of his feelings.

Hamlet's logical and emotional uncertainty at the beginning of his fourth—or second major—soliloquy (II, ii, 575–634) is the result of his inability to explore fully a "Cause" which must be known fully before it can have a logical "Effect." The King's villainy, as a Cause outside Hamlet's self, is still not self-evident; and the Prince, for the moment, can only look into himself for the "Internal Causes" which may affect his condition without "efficiently" determining it—even though he knows that his cue for passion is much greater than that of the player whose exhibition he has just been witnessing. Systematically, his first consideration is of his "Form" or inner spirit. He calls himself a dull and muddy-mettled rascal, peak,

like John-a-dreams unpregnant of his cause, and he logically goes on to ask whether his "Matter" might not be
that of a coward. It cannot be but that he is pigeon-livered,
and lacks gall, he suggests. The text of the 1603 Quarto
(which reads "why sure I am a coward . . . or else I have
no gall") is more explicit in dichotomizing "Form" and
"Matter," but in either version it is evident that Hamlet is
not satisfied with self-analysis as a complete exploration
of "Cause." The King's guilt must be made evident before
the investigation is complete, and at the end of the soliloquy he proposes the device of the play which will serve
his logical purpose.

In the meantime, however, he has explored the first
logical Arguments with sufficient thoroughness to proceed
down the table and ask whether his own state of mind or
whether revenge itself should be the proper "Subject" of
his meditations. The question, as he settles it in the same
soliloquy, is hardly arguable. "Vengeance" is his spontaneous exclamation as he thinks of that bloody, bawdy vil-
lain, his uncle, and he begins to consider himself as a mere
"Adjunct" to the "Subject" revenge in which his scullion
self should be "occupied." He remains acutely aware of
the dubious value of the ghost's testimony, considering
the possibility that it might be the testimony of an evil
spirit in disguise; but when he bids his brain to turn about
and plan the means of catching the conscience of the King
he is thinking from a new point of view—not from a sub-
jective regard for his own state of mind but from a tentative
acceptance of the necessity of revenge.

But was this necessity real? Hamlet had explored the
table of "Agreeable" Arguments, but logic also offered a
table of "Disagreeable" ones beginning with a consideration of the most clearly determined alternatives. To be, or
not to be—that was the new question which logical pro-
gression offered for meditation in his next soliloquy (III,

i, 56–88). He could live and either suffer the slings and arrows of outrageous fortune or else take arms against his sea of troubles and by opposing end them. Or he could do the opposite, die and with the sleep of death end the heartache and the thousand natural shocks his flesh was heir to. Surely here was a perfect logical "Contrary" or mutually exclusive choice. But the phrase "to be, or not to be," as Abraham Fraunce had already pointed out, did not represent a mutually exclusive alternative, for "not to be" was a statement which could be either affirmed or (on the grounds of a belief after death) denied. Hamlet's mind worked in the same direction. The thought of death as a sleep, in which dreams perchance might come, gave him pause. Life might not be "Contrary" to death but simply "Disparate" from it. Or the two states might not be "Opposites" at all but merely "Divers" or "somewhat differing" in their nature. Here was an Argument which could not be explored—the sort that puzzles the will and makes us rather bear those ills we have than fly to others that we know not of. The only real choice was that involved in living—the choice between active enterprises of great pith and moment and an inactive suffering which was not nobility of mind but an intellectually sicklied shade of native resolution.

Hamlet's "to be, or not to be" meditation, in short, cleared the way for the decision in his sixth soliloquy (III, ii, 407–18)—after the successful experiment of the play and the clarification of his primary "Cause"—that his too-logical self should be occupied in active revenge: at the witching hour of night he could do such bitter business as the day would quake to look upon so long as it was not unnatural. By this time the "Inartificial" Argument of the ghost's testimony had been supported by the "Artificial" or self-evident Argument of the King's guilty behavior, and nothing stood between the Prince and his revenge except opportunity and the dangling ends of "Compared" Arguments with which Fenner's primary table concluded.

When the first opportunity arose, Hamlet seized it—to continue his progress through the table. A better occasion than the discovery of the King at prayer, in fact, could hardly have been designed for the purpose of enabling him to scan the formal Argument of "Quantity" which was next on the logical list. Through it he had to discover whether the injury he would do the King was "Equal" or "Greater" or "Less" than that which the king had done his father, and he required little meditation (III, iii, 73–96) to reach the conclusion that killing the King while he was purging of his royal soul would be a lesser injury than that done the elder Hamlet when he was taken with his crimes full blown. To make his revenge "Equal" to or "Greater" than the thing revenged Hamlet would have to put up his sword until he could catch his uncle in some act that had no relish of salvation in it and so trip him into hell.

By this time Hamlet was through with indecision and should have been past the necessity for further soliloquizing. But one more division of Fenner's primary Arguments—a comparison of "Quality," "Unlike" and "Like"— remained to be explored. And in his eighth and final soliloquy (IV, iv, 32–66) Hamlet went through with this final Argument, completing the process of dividing and subdividing, dichotomizing and quartering his thoughts in accord with a logical system. A man was unlike a beast, designed to do nothing more than sleep and feed, for his discursive reason had been given him for use. Whether the Prince had used his own reason too poorly and sunk into bestial oblivion or whether he had used it to the cowardly excess of thinking too precisely on the event he did not know. As a man, he was like young Fortinbras and his followers, who set him an example by being ready to expose what was mortal and unsure to all that fortune, death, and danger dare for less reason than he had found for action. His own case had been thoroughly explored through the entire table of logical "Invention" and all its implications had been "discovered." He had found "great argument"—more than adequate "Cause" or "Reason"— to stir in defense of his honor. He had no more need for the guidance offered by logical "Invention" and could at last proceed to the orderly "Disposition" of his further thoughts. Since he had no public to persuade, he had no occasion to use any of the elaborate Ramean or Scholastic methods. His announced but undemonstrated method was the simplest that Fenner recommended—the axiomatic: "O, from this time forth, My thoughts be bloody, or be nothing worth!"

V

When I first made this analysis almost twenty years ago and thought it interesting enough for submission to a scholarly journal, I found that I should have taken Abraham Fraunce's warning to heart. One editor who was also a professional Shakespearean had the kindness to take me into his office, close the door, and warn me that I was very "unwise" to let my mind dwell on Peter Ramus—whose influence during the Renaissance was, in his opinion, "terribly exaggerated." A distinguished editor of Shakespeare, serving as a reader for another journal, rejected it flatly with the indignant comment: the author "can make a Ramist out of Polonius if he wants to, but he cannot do this to Hamlet!" And a professional logician, acting as a consultant for still another editor, put both Ramus and me in our places with the observation that logic was traditionally concerned with demonstration and an emphasis upon invention reflected an inadequate grasp of the subject.

Yet it seems to me that Shakespeare has withstood enough nonsense over the centuries to be able to bear up under the possibility of a little more and that the ghost of Ramus haunts the soliloquies whether or not one is inclined to believe in such spirits. In any case, it was never my intention to commit lese majesty against the Royal Dane. If Hamlet was a Ramist, Shakespeare made him so and made Polonius the parody of a Scholastic; and if Hamlet's primary concern was with deciding rather than with convincing somebody that a decision was just, that fact reflects nothing more than the difference between the freedom of a creative dramatist and the responsibilities of a professor of philosophy. My own position, as I see it, is that of the innocent beholder who is perhaps sticking his neck out too far in an effort to see something new beneath the surface of one of the most ambiguous, intellectually teasing, and variously interpreted masterpieces of all literature.

For that reason I am not inclined to stress the possible importance of this alleged logic to an understanding of Shakespeare, the plot of the play, or the character of its hero. I may doubt whether the question of an author's belief or disbelief in ghosts is relevant to literary criticism, suspect that the play within the play has a logical place in the plot, and cherish the opinion that Hamlet was not represented as a person so irrational in his behavior that he can be understood only through psychoanalysis; but I do not care to see the play sicklied over with another pale cast of thought. Least of all do I want to suggest that Shakespeare was a Ramist in some way intellectually akin to Gabriel Harvey. The pattern of thought surveyed here seems to be almost unique in his plays. It is peculiar to *Hamlet* and to the soliloquies—so much so, in fact, that I am sometimes tempted to pacify the shakers and quakers among our modern editors by allying myself with the "firey-faced" Aristotelians of an earlier day and suggesting that a university term and a freshman's fascination with "new fangled" logic may have provided the tragic flaw in Hamlet's otherwise noble character. But I prefer to be neutral with reference to Shakespeare's possible intent. The analogy I have observed may provide another illustration of the dramatist's comprehensive grasp of his time, or it may be—if the professional Shakespeareans will have it so— simply a provoking rather than a provocative coincidence.

CHAPTER SIX

In Rightly Dividing
the Word of Truth:
Ramean Hermeneutics
and the Commandment
Against Adultery*

I

Because Peter Ramus was a Protestant martyr and a rebel against Scholasticism, his logic has always been associated with the Reformation and, in England, especially with the Puritans, who found it particularly adaptable to the exegesis of biblical texts. To them the Word of God had superseded the Church as the supreme authority in their lives; and the Bible, as the historical revelation of the word, was their most important source of knowledge. It had to be interpreted rationally and in accord with some readily understood system if it was to guide the mass of men whose learning was small but whose equal responsibility to God compelled them to be independent of any authority above and beyond their common understanding. Not all were called to be interpreters, as the apostle Paul had made

*The substance of this has been used orally on various occasions, but the essay has not been published.

It should be followed by an account of the Puritans' use of the "Second Part of Logic" in their "Disposition" of Arguments in a way which would make doctrines privately "Invented" or "Discovered" appear convincing to other persons. But this properly belongs elsewhere, and if I ever manage to get together the fragments of an unfinished study of the Puritans some consideration of Puritan preaching will be included in it.

clear; but every flock should have its shepherd, and in England good shepherds were notoriously scarce.

Roland MacIlmaine, from the University of St. Andrews in Scotland, probably had this in mind when he published the first translation of Ramus's *Logic* into English in London in 1574. His introductory Epistle shows his concern for the need to teach "the worde of God truly" without the "trickes of poysonable sophistrie" and the beguilements of ancient authors, for he asked the "gentle reader" to call "upon god that it wyll please his heaunlie Maiestie to plante this our rule of veritie in the hartes of all men, but most chieflie in the breastes of the Pastors of the Churche, who have the charge and dispensation of his holye worde."[1] The effectiveness and influence of his work, however, remains unknown.

For the appearance of MacIlmaine's *The Logicke of Peter Ramus* was untimely. The "Exercises" designed to train ministers skilled in the interpretation of the Scriptures, which were begun in Northampton in 1571, had spread throughout the country; and in the year MacIlmaine's book appeared they came to the attention of Queen Elizabeth who ordered them suppressed in the Diocese of Norwich and began her campaign to suppress uncontrolled preaching (or prophesying, as it was then called) throughout the country. Two years later all licenses to preach dated before February 8, 1575, were declared void;[2] and if all the bishops had been severe about issuing new licenses, preaching would have been limited to strict conformists and brought under complete control. But it was not until the new Archbishop of Canterbury, Edmund Grindal, had been sequestered for supporting the practice of prophesying and made his submission in 1577, that the training Exercises were entirely suppressed (I, 359). A survey made in 1586 showed that only about one-fifth of the churches in England had preaching ministers, and Dudley Fenner, an aggressive young Puritan curate, estimated that a third of the ministers in England were "covered with a Cloud of Suspensions" (as he himself was). Fenner also claimed that in many places a person wanting to hear a sermon might have to travel from five to twenty miles to do so and risk being fined for absence from services in his own parish if he did. Many of those who were licensed to preach apparently did not do so, for in that same year the Bishop of London taxed his clergy the price of four purchased sermons a year if they did not deliver their own (I, 479).

This did not mean that preaching disappeared as completely as the records suggest. But it does mean that many of the curates and lecturers who had done much of the preaching for incompetent or absentee holders of clerical livings were careful not to call attention to themselves and did not gather together for exercises which would improve their gifts and encourage others to emulate them. Preaching was simply not a publicly cultivated art during the decade before the threat of foreign invasion lessened some of the internal conflicts which divided English Protestants.

During this decade Dudley Fenner published in Holland his own version of Ramus in *The Arts of Logike and Rhetorike plainely set forth in the English tongue* (Middleburgh, 1584) which was peculiarly adapted to biblical exegesis insomuch as the section on logic ignored the first or efficient cause and enabled the expositor to begin, as MacIlmaine had advised, with the text he had "taken in hand to interprete" (p. 7). There is no more evidence of the immediate influence of Fenner's logic than there is of MacIlmaine's, but it was reprinted in the same year and again in 1588. These three printings would have more than supplied the needs of the English preachers in Holland, and numerous copies were probably smuggled into England. The only other version of Ramus available in English during the sixteenth century was Abraham Fraunce's

The Lawiers Logike, which placed a much greater emphasis upon varieties of causation. It was first issued and reprinted twice in 1588.

The first clear connection between the logic of Ramus and biblical exegesis, however, was in William Perkins's *Prophetica, sive de saora et vnica ratione concionandi,* which was published and reprinted in Cambridge in 1592 and translated into English by Thomas Tuke in 1606 under the title *The Arte of Prophecying, or, A Treatise concerning the onely trve manner and methode of Preaching.* As W. S. Howell observed, Perkins carefully dichotomized the treatment of his subject, and, Howell added, "This prevailingly dichotomous structure is of course Ramistic, and so far as I know, Perkins is the first Englishman to write of preaching in terms of that kind of structure." According to Howell's well-informed judgment, though, Perkins was not a "thoroughgoing disciple" of Ramus. He did not mention Ramus among his authorities but, instead, "derives his doctrine from sources closer to Ciceronian rhetoric and scholastic logic than to the logic and rhetoric of Ramus."[3]

Nevertheless, in laying down his principles of exegesis, Perkins appeared to be a throughgoing Ramist. He made a Ramistic division between the art of preparing a sermon and that of uttering it, and he divided preparation into two parts: "interpretation and right division or cutting." The first of these consisted of discovering "one entire and natural sense" in "the words and sentences of the scripture," and Perkins followed Ramus's attempt to avoid confusion between the arts of logic and rhetoric (as well as the principles of most non-Lutheran protestants) by rejecting Catholic "allegorical, tropological, and anagogical" meanings in favor of complete concern for the "literal." "There is only one sense and the same is the literal," he said. "An allegory is only a certain manner of uttering the same sense, the anagoge and tropology are ways whereby the sense may be applied."[4]

When he turned to what he called "the right dividing of the word," Perkins was more explicit in his Ramism. This phrase was derived from Paul's advice to Timothy, which read, in the Geneva Bible: "Studie to shewe thy self approued vnto God, a workeman that nedeth not to be ashamed, diuiding the worde of trueth aright." The Geneva editors had first annotated the concluding phrase as "Giuing to euerie one his iuste portion" and later as "By adding nothing to it, neither over stepping any thing, neither mangling it, nor renting it in sunder: but marking dilligently what his hearers are able to heare, and what is fit for edifying."[5] Both of these annotations referred to the act of preaching, but Perkins, whose mind was on exegesis, was concerned with the way "doctrine not expressed" might be "soundly gathered out of the text." "This is done," he said, "by the help of the nine arguments, that is of the causes, effects, subjects, adjuncts, dissentaries, comparatives, names, distribution and definition" (p. 340). These "nine arguments," as Perkins stated them, were from Ramus's original logic rather than from that of any of his English followers; and, as Howell observed, "Perkins was thinking of that very work when he penned this passage" (p. 207).

II

What a person might be thinking of in the private act of gathering doctrine out of a particular text, however, is not so easy to determine. The first six of Perkins's "nine arguments" are what Ramus had called "simple" or primary arguments, and these were the ones English Ramists emphasized as the most trustworthy to be used in reasoning with one's self in an attempt to discover "truth" before presenting it to an audience which might require a quite different method of persuasion. The use of these "arguments" becomes unmistakable only when the attempt to persuade others is combined with a disclosure of the intellectual processes used by the preacher or teacher to persuade himself that his doctrines were soundly gathered.

A rare (and, so far as I know, unique) example of such combination is in a book by Perkins's older contemporary, Thomas Cartwright, which was first published in 1611, eight years after his death, and again in 1616 as *A Treatise of Christian Religion, or the whole Bodie and Substance of Divinitie.* The treatise was in the form of a catechism, questions and answers, obviously devised for the simplest of understandings; but each chapter was preceded by a table of dichotomies showing more intellectual readers how the doctrine had been soundly gathered. Even in these tables Cartwright did not reveal all the private reasoning he must have used to produce them. He used only those formal "Arguments" which suited his purpose in each particular chapter, extending or modifying the system as all Ramists did, and adapting his terminology to a clear statement of his inferences. Also, in its lack of concern for first and final causes, his system resembled Fenner's rather than that of Ramus or any of his other followers. The two men were closely associated in Antwerp and later at Middelburg (where Fenner died at the age of about twenty-nine in 1587), and the distinctive form of Fenner's own system may, in fact, have been determined by discussions with his older and more learned friend and colleague.

Cartwright's resemblance to Fenner in his treatment of causation may be briefly indicated by his consideration of the Fall of Man.[6] The causes of the Fall were of two sorts: (1) External (of which the principal cause was Satan and the instrument was the serpent) and (2) Internal, which was subdivided into "corporall" (i.e., "material"), consisting of the physical acts of seeing, touching, and tasting, and "mental" (i.e., "spiritual" or "formal") displayed as "appetite." There was no consideration of "First" or "Final" causes. God and his Providence were not matters to be explored by reason but accepted by faith. Since the story of the temptation had been clearly set forth in the scriptures, Cartwright was constrained to go beyond the Ramean logical pattern by dealing briefly with the "Manner" of the Fall, showing that "the woman did first eat" and the man "by her persuasion"; but he had no Miltonic compulsion to "justify the ways of God to men" by dealing elaborately with the events which, traditionally, led up to the original sin.

For textual exegesis per se, however, the question of cause usually did not arise. Human reason did not raise it when contemplating the revealed Word of God—especially when the Word was supposed to come directly from God rather than from one of his followers. Nevertheless, the pattern of thought which included an analysis of causation often appeared in explications which did not deal specifically with the idea itself. The shadow of Ramus, in short, can be frequently seen when the substance of his system appears to be missing; and a good illustration of this may be found in one of Cartwright's most exhaustive uses of Ramean analysis in "discovering" a variety of doctrines in one short text with a simple literal meaning. The text is Exodus 20, 14: "Thou shalt not commit adultery," which the editors of the Geneva Bible consistently annotated as a command to "be pure in heart, word, and deed," and in which Cartwright found all this and much more.

It formed Chapter 22, "Of the seventh Commandment," of his *Treatise* and was introduced by a diagram which related it to other "Things belonging to our Neighbour" and dealt with adultery itself as follows:

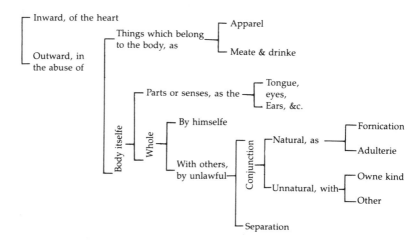

When this chart is compared with the one derived from Dudley Fenner, it becomes evident that while Cartwright used a similar system of dichotomies he did not use Fenner's logical terminology. Nor does he appear to use at all the dichotomies of Fenner's first set of "Agreeable" Arguments—Cause and Effect—which were usually so important in the Ramean system. This should not be surprising. There was no reason to apply any elaborate ideas of causation to a consideration of the Ten Commandments. They represented God's law, given to Moses as a direct expression of his will. Some of the sins they forbade, such as covetousness, might be traced back to Adam; but the Commandments, as a whole, were directed against acts over which even sinful man was expected to have some control, and any reasons man might offer for violating them were as irrelevant in God's eyes as God's reasons for giving them were in the eyes of man. The Ramean question "Why?" was not pertinent to God's direct commands or man's obligation to obey them.

In another way, a consideration of the effects of this Commandment and the disobedience of it was also irrelevant to this diagram. Because the primary purpose of *A Treatise on Christian Divinity* was to gather doctrine by rightly dividing the Word, it generally provided material for that part of a sermon which was conventionally labeled "Doctrine." The application or "Use" of it was left up to the individual preacher facing a particular congregation. Nevertheless, Cartwright occasionally provided suggestions as to how it could be used. He did so in this instance in the very last paragraph of the chapter in response to the question "What are the punishments of the [Commandment's] breach?" These included not only the judgment of God upon the offender and the Mosaic injunction against admitting bastards ("to the tenth generation") into the Sanctuary but such physical punishments as whipping for fornication and "death to other unlawful mixtures." "And children begotten in horrible incest," he added in the last sentence, "were to be burnt or slaine in their mothers wombe" (pp. 146–47). Adultery, he pointed out, was one of the most commonly discovered crimes, and the effects of its commission could be terrifying.

III

Despite what seems to have been adequate reasons for ignoring Fenner's table of Agreeable Arguments, however, a closer examination of Cartwright's chart shows that he actually used part of it. Apparently assuming that adultery, as a sin for which man could be held responsible, had an Internal rather than an External Cause, he divided it into two categories, Inward and Outward, which corresponded to the traditional "Formal" and "Material" Causes. These corresponded with the everyday Christian dichotomy of

Soul and Body and the special Puritan concern for sin in
spirit as well as in deed. Though these were not strictly
causal ideas, they reflect the same pattern of thought and
so enable us to visualize a relationship between the treatise
on logic and that on religion by imposing a parenthetical
commentary on Cartwright upon a diagram derived from
Fenner:

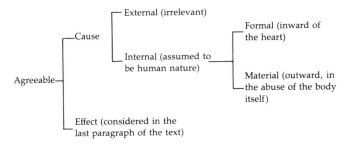

In contrast to his rather tenuous use of the first table,
Cartwright adopted Fenner's second table of "Less Agreeable" Arguments quite obviously, though with some revisions and additions. This table was based upon a
distinction between the "Subject" (or "the body itself") and
its "Adjuncts" (or "things which belong to the body"), and
he treated the less important Adjuncts first. These he divided, with external and internal dichotomy still in his
mind, into "Apparel" on the one hand and "meate and
drinke" on the other. As he explained in his text, a person
could commit adultery in his apparel by wearing clothes
which belonged to the opposite sex or which were wan-
tonly alluring, contrary to the custom of one's community,
or "new-fangled." Meat and drink could be adulterous
either in quality "when wee seeke after too much daintiness" or in quantity "when we feed to fulness of them"
(pp. 141–42).

The Subject was "Body itselfe," and Cartwright's treatment of it is especially interesting because it took him

beyond Fenner's version of the Ramean system and even beyond Ramus himself as he made use of certain ideas which seem to have been derived from Abraham Fraunce's *The Lawiers Logike* and its treatment of the Efficient Cause in its various modes of operation. One of these is to be found in his distinction between the "Whole" body and its "Parts," the latter being interpreted as the "Senses" and more specifically as those of the tongue and ear (such as producing or listening to "bad songs, ballads, interludes, amorous books, and such like") and those of the eye ("which is the seate of adulterie") in beholding "the beautie of another, or the wanton pictures and the like things, that the heart is inflamed to lust thereby" (p. 143). Another causal dichotomy was a man's mode of committing adultery "By himselfe" and "With others." The first consisted of "ceasing from doing any profitable thing, as in Idlenesse. Or by the horrible sin of *Onan* and the like pollutions" (p. 144). The second mode was more complicated, and will be continued after this second illustration of Cartwright's use of a logical table:

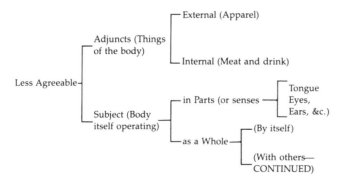

Since Cartwright treated as "Parts" of the body not only the perceptive senses of hearing and sight but such actions as singing and talking and (in his expository text) such complete bodily motions as those involved in "wanton

dancing and such laciuious motions" (p. 144), it is evident
that by "the body itself" he meant the sexual organs; and
to the misuse of these he applied the whole of Fenner's
analysis of "Disagreeable" Arguments, involving both differences and comparisons. He did not, however, follow
Fenner in using separate tables for his "Differences" and
"Comparisons." Instead, he incorporated the second into
the first and used explicit and implicit comparisons to illustrate the different ways adultery could be committed
both in "Conjunction" and in "Separation." Because of the
complexity of this rearrangement and also because some
of Cartwright's notions about adulterous separation are
unusual if not unique, it may be desirable in this instance
to present the visual comparison before commenting upon
it.

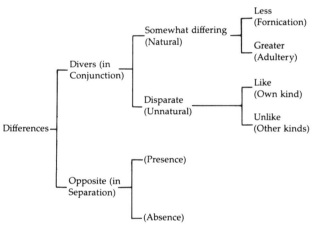

Unlawful conjunction could be either "Natural" or "Unnatural," corresponding to the "Somewhat differing" and
"Disparate" Arguments of Dudley Fenner. Unlawful natural conjunction could be either fornication or adultery.
Although the Puritans made no distinction between mortal and venial sins, all sin being equal in the eyes of God,

they did make a distinction between crimes; and it was therefore appropriate that the "Comparative" Arguments of "Greater" and "Less" be applied to this kind of sexual misbehavior. As a crime committed against one's neighbor, fornication (punishable only by whipping) was obviously the lesser of the two, and adultery (punishable by death) was the greater. The Comparative Arguments of Quality, "Like" and "Unlike," were similarly attached to "Unnatural" Conjunction, which might be with "One's own kind" or with "Other kinds"—that is, abnormal sexual relations with man or beasts. Cartwright did not mention them in his paragraph on punishments, but under the Puritan laws of Massachusetts Bay they were both punishable by death.

The most extraordinary section of the analysis is the last in which Cartwright presented a concept of adultery which was neither "Inward" nor "Outward" and was absolutely "Contrary" to adultery by any form of "Conjunction." This was adultery by "Separation" which could occur in the additionally opposite states of "Presence" or "Absence." It could be committed "when the partie is present" "When due[7] beneuolence is not yeelded, although there bee aptnesse thereunto, nor any hinderance by consent, in respect of extraordinarie prayer" (p. 146). This doctrine was taken from I Corinthians 7. 3–5, which Cartwright not only echoed but cited in a marginal note:

> Let the housband give vnto the wife due beneuolence, and likewise the wife vnto the housband.
>
> The wife hathe not ye power of her owne boddie, but the housband: and likewise also the housband hathe not the power of his owne bodie, but the wife.
>
> Defraude not one another, except it be with consent for a time, that ye may giue your selues to fasting and prayer, & againe come together that Satan tempt you not for your incontinencie.

And, despite the obscurity of Cartwright's last ten words, his teaching was probably intended to be in accord with the context of this passage. Paul had preceded it with the assertion that "It were good[8] for a man not to touche a woman" but that nevertheless every man should have a wife and every woman a husband in order "to avoid fornication." Furthermore, he had added that he spoke this "by permission, not by commandment." Cartwright's teaching differed substantially from Paul's in that it represented the sexual relationship of marriage not as a permitted and legalized means for avoiding sin but as something directly commanded by God. Any refusal, except by mutual consent under extraordinary circumstances, was a form of adultery in itself and therefore a violation of the Seventh Commandment.

This concept of what might be called "negative adultery"—that is, continence forced upon a married person—also pervaded Cartwright's consideration of Separation by Absence. Of this he simply said that adultery occurred "when the partie withdraweth itselfe, in mislike, or loathsomenesse; or else by long and vnnecessary journeyes of trauelling, of merchandize, warres, &c. Or when separation hath been made by the Magistrate, without lawful cause" (p. 146). This is an unusual expression of Puritan sympathy for the woman, for, although either partner in marriage might experience mislike or loathing for the other and neither could be held responsible for arbitrary acts of the Magistrate, the man was the usual offender when separation occurred as a result of unnecessary travelling, merchandizing, and war. Such examples as these probably reflect sixteenth-century social conditions which we will consider later, but, for the moment, it is only necessary to observe that they offer an insight into a Puritan attitude toward sexual relationship which is not often considered.

Cartwright's analysis of the Seventh Commandment is

one of his most extraordinary extrapolations of a biblical text and perhaps the best example available of the ingenuity with which the whole of the Ramean "Arguments" could be adapted to "the right dividing of the word" in systematic scriptural exegesis. To the five simple words of the Commandment, which apparently had a straightforward literal meaning, he applied all the relevant Arguments of Dudley Fenner's logical textbook and to them added others probably derived from Abraham Fraunce's more sophisticated *Lawiers Logike*. By doing so, he was able to derive from it a harmony of doctrine which brought together a variety of other biblical passages and so provided the rationale for a number of Puritan practices in appearance, behavior, and attitude for which there were no specific biblical injunctions. The most striking effect of Ramean logic upon his mind, however, was in the rational assurance which enabled him to transform the apostle Paul's permissive attitude toward marriage into a positive command from God and to insist upon the moral obligation of each individual to satisfy the relationships involved in the union of two people in one flesh.

IV

Cartwright was writing at a crucial time in English history when the Puritans were relatively inactive but were on the verge of their aggressive outburst under the Stuart kings. It is therefore difficult to know when he was reflecting the historical forces of the sixteenth century or anticipating and perhaps influencing those of the seventeenth. But marriage was a matter which was not only of importance to the Puritans but one which had strongly affected the clergy from the beginning of the Reformation. Most of the leading Protestant ministers had taken wives soon after they separated from Rome; and Elizabeth, who was strongly opposed to a married clergy and tried to keep clerical wives off ecclesiastical premises at the beginning of her reign, had been forced to control her prejudices in order to consolidate her power. Many Anglican clergymen who may have had little interest in preserving the Reformation were concerned about the preservation of their marital state and the legitimacy of their children.[9] Furthermore, at a time when the profits of the woolen trade were causing the transformation of farms into pastures and hordes of displaced persons were moving to London, family stability offered the only defense against social chaos. Cartwright's teaching was a stronger and more positive doctrine than that generally attributed to the Puritans, who are supposed, in popular tradition at least, to have been so opposed to the enjoyment of sexual relations that they were hypocritical about the marriage relationship.

This has also affected the attitude of well-informed historians that is represented perhaps as well as it is anywhere else by M. M. Knappen in his study of *Tudor Puritanism*.[10] There he bases the Puritan attitude toward marriage upon Paul's assertion "It is better to marry than to burn" and adds that, though "divinely ordained," it was "Not ordained for the pure enjoyment of mankind . . . but only as a remedy for lust." Yet it was "only *a* remedy," he continued with emphasis. A better remedy was celibacy—"the gift of having no necessity [for sexual relations], a blessing conferred by a special act of God's grace" (p. 452). This view was widely taught and preached, as Knappen's citations prove, but it was not "the whole body and substance" of Christian doctrine as taught by Thomas Cartwright.

Knappen introduced his account of the Puritan theory of marriage by a reference to "the general Protestant assault on the Catholic doctrine of celibacy" which, carried to its "logical conclusion," he said, "would have been to esteem the married state at least as high as the celibate, as one of the good gifts of God, provided for man's aid and comfort" and implied that the Puritans "qualified" their logic by assuming that the virtues of marriage were in the companionship of "a pleasant helpmeet" (pp. 451–52). There was no such qualification in Cartwright's *Treatise*. It taught that sexual intercourse in marriage, whenever there as "an aptnesse thereunto" by either party, was a duty required by God's commandment. A violation of this duty, either by illegal intercourse or abstinence without mutual consent, was sin against divine law. I suspect that this was a doctrine more widely held than preached because it was considered one of the matters unseemly to be spoken of plainly in public. However this may be, it helps explain why the Puritans could strongly support marriage as a social institution while continuing to hold the Protestant conviction that it was not a sacrament. Although ordained for man in this life because of his imperfections (or, as Milton was later to put it, his "deficiencie"), marriage need not be maintained when he achieved his perfect existence in heaven nor should it be maintained on earth when it failed to achieve its purpose. It legalized and symbolized the union of man and woman in one flesh, not in one spirit, and if this physical union could not be preserved in fact, it should be dissolved.

Another doctrine of special historical interest refers to what Knappen called "such indifferent matters as food and drink" (p. 453). They were not indifferent to Cartwright. By his reasoning, they (as well as intemperance in apparel and bawdiness in speaking, hearing, and seeing) were violations of the Seventh Commandment and, as such, positive sins. His introduction into his system of "such things that belong to the body" as apparel, meat, and drink, in fact, provides a better example than sex of the carryover of medieval Catholic morality into the ethical system that Knappen finds characteristic of the Puritans. For by this means Cartwright managed to make Pride and Gluttony, even though there was no specific biblical injunction against them, forms of Lust and therefore the Deadly Sins they had been in medieval times.

Cartwright knew, however, that civil law did not proscribe those things which he considered sinful abuses of things belonging to the body or such parts of the body as the senses, and so he went to unusual lengths in explaining what he considered morally legal. Clothing should clearly reveal God's distinction between the sexes and should be designed to please but not to "allure" a member of the opposite sex. It should also be modest and decent and "according to the custome of the country, citie, or towne where wee dwell" rather than "new-fangled" (pp. 141–42). In food and drink, he recommended "a modest and sober diet" (p. 142). On ordinary occasions for speech, a person could avoid violation of the commandment by "modest and chaste talke" and at other times by following "the example of the holy Ghost, who speaking (by necessity) of matters vnseemly to be spoken plainly of, vseth chast speech" (p. 143). His final admonitions were against a person's "delighting in hearing vnhonest and filthie words, although (for his credit) hee will not speake them" and against abuse of other parts of the body by "light gesture & behauiour" and by "wanton dancing and other lasciuious motions" (pp. 143–44). Later in the seventeenth century all of these teachings became incorporated in Puritan manners and custom and some of them into the sumptuary laws of the Massachusetts Bay Colony.

The third doctrine of special historical interest which Cartwright drew out of this text is the most far-fetched and puzzling, possibly because it was related to his personal observation of Puritan tribulations in sixteenth-century England. This was the doctrine of adultery in unnecessary travelling, merchandizing, and war, and especially "when separation hath been made by the Magistrate without lawful cause." This clearly referred to the separation itself as a sin rather than to any adulterous thought or act that might be caused by it. To Cartwright such separations were all too familiar. For he was, as his biographer puts it, "a much travelled man"[11] who had been a chaplain in Ireland and who had experienced involuntary exile in Geneva, and again in Heidelberg and Basel, among the English merchandizers in Middelburg and Antwerp, and finally in Leyden. And after his own late marriage, at the age of forty-two in March 1577–78, he suffered imprisonment for two long years.

The circumstances surrounding his own imprisonment probably called forth the last and most remarkable of his examples of adultery in separation—remarkable because of its reference to the unlawful act of "the Magistrate" in the singular instead of "Magistrates" in general, and because it is the only instance in this chapter which attributes an explicit External Cause to the sin he discusses. The impertinence of the Martin Marprelate pamphlets had aroused the Queen to a systematic enquiry into the nonconformist practices of both the clergy and laity throughout England. It resulted in a number of arrests, including that of the Reverend John Udal, who, in what seems to have been a notoriously unfair trial, was sentenced to death on the suspicion of libel. More prominent Puritans, including Cartwright, who disclaimed any association with libelous pamphleteers were also arrested, jailed, and tried before the Queen's High Commission for ecclesiastical affairs and the Star Chamber, which represented her personal authority and power. During this whole period, from 1590 to 1592, Elizabeth was constantly asserting her authority over all ecclesiastical cases, and Parliament's acceptance of her assertion was considered by the Puritans an extraordinary submission of traditional English liberty to "Acts of sovereign power which none of her Majesty's Ancestors assumed."[12] Because of illness and the influence of powerful friends, and on the promise of quiet and peaceful behavior, Cartwright was released from the Fleet in 1592 and restored to his position as governor of a hospital in Warwick. He retired to the island of Guernsey in 1595, where he remained for six of the last eight years of his life and probably composed his *Treatise*. It is not surprising that the book remained in manuscript during the Queen's lifetime.

There was, then, more than simple logic in Cartwright's exegesis of the commandment against adultery. By means of the extrapolation used in Ramean Invention he was able to "discover" in the five words of the commandment an injunction of sorts against the medieval sins of Pride and Gluttony, a rationale for the Puritan plainness in dress and diet, a basis for the Puritan opposition to the wantonness of plays and pastimes, an argument against "ceasing from doing any profitable thing, as in Idlenesse," and a doctrine which supported family stability and a conception of marriage based upon human love rather than the fear of sin. Some of the inferences he drew undoubtedly reflected the prejudices and problems of the times. The practice of enclosure and the consequent migration of great numbers of displaced country people to London placed increasing stress upon the family as a stabilizing institution and made the marriage upon which it was based an object of social as well as religious concern. The growing popularity of the stage made plays the rival of sermons as an attraction for large audiences, and it probably pleased Puritans to discover that, while the latter were frequently condemned by the State, the former were doubly damned by the Lord because of the bawdiness of the comic interludes and the sex-confusion created by male actors in female roles. And it is probable, too, that the Puritans found satisfaction in the belief that the pains of exile and imprisonment, which so many of them suffered for conscience's sake, were not misfortunes but a positive sin which was being forced upon them and which they could legitimately resist. The motivation which lay behind this example of Puritan hermeneutics, however, is only a matter for speculation. The observable fact is that the Ramean system of logic enabled a representative Puritan to go far beyond the literal meaning of the scriptures without engaging in the Roman practice of allegorizing them.

Notes

1. Roland MacIlmaine, *The Logike of the Most Excellent Philosopher P. Ramus Martyr,* ed. Catherine M. Dunn (Northridge, California: San Fernando Valley State College Renaissance Editions, 1969), p. 5. When the reference is clear, further citations to this and to other sources will be made by page number within the text.

2. Daniel Neal, *The History of the Puritans* (London, 1732), I, 343. An account of the Exercises in prophesying is given on pp. 273–77 and of their suppression on p. 327.

3. Wilbur Samuel Howell, *Logic and Rhetoric in England, 1500–1700* (Princeton, New Jersey: Princeton University Press, 1956), pp. 206–7.

4. Although my original notes are from the London, 1631 edition of Perkins's *Works,* the quotations are all in the abbreviated edition of *The Work of William Perkins,* ed. Ian Breward in *The Courtenay Library of Reformation Classics* (Appleford, Abingdon, Berkshire, England: The Sutton Courtenay Press, n.d.), pp. 337–38.

5. I have used the University of Wisconsin Press facsimile copy of the first (1560) edition and my own copy of a London, 1599 edition, of which there are variant copies with the same title page. The biblical quotation is 2 Timothy. 2. 15, as it was printed in the 1560 edition.

6. The *Treatise* was probably composed during Cartwright's residence in Guernsey (1595–1601) after he had promised to refrain from controversy. My quotations are from the London, 1616 edition. I have not seen a copy of the 1611 edition, and none is listed in the *STC*. Cartwright deals with the Fall in Chapter 9, pp. 42 ff. Further references are by page within the text.

7. The note on "due" in the first edition of the Geneva Bible reads: "Which conteineth all due ties perteining to marriage." That in the last is: "This word (due) conteineth all kind of benevolence, though he speake more of one sort then of the other, in that that followeth."

8. In the first edition of the Geneva Bible the word "good" is annotated as meaning "expedient," because, as the note goes on to explain, "mariage, through mans corruption, and not by Gods institution bringeth cares and troubles." This annotation does not appear in the last edition.

9. A. G. Dickens has a good (and well-indexed) discussion of clerical marriage in *The English Reformation* (New York: Schocken Books, 1964). His opinion is that "this matter of clerical marriage bulked large" in the early stages of the English Reformation (p. 245) although it was "a poor index to Protestant convictions" (p. 278).

10. Originally published in 1930. My quotations are from the University of Chicago Press reprint in 1970.

11. A. F. Scott Pearson, *Thomas Cartwright and Elizabethan Puritanism 1535–1603* (Cambridge University Press, 1925), p. 54. This has been the source of all my biographical information about Cartwright.

12. Neal, *The History of the Puritans,* I, 541. I have used Neal's account of these events (I, 503 ff.) as representative of the Puritan view of them. The best and most unbiased account, based upon exhaustive research, is by Patrick Collinson, *The Elizabethan Puritan Movement* (University of California Press: Berkeley and Los Angeles, 1967), pp. 417–31. The basic question of the queen's legal authority in ecclesiastical cases is mentioned on pp. 420–21.

CHAPTER SEVEN

In Pleading and in Planning: Portia's Reasoning and a Lawyer's Light on Professional Logic*

I
Portia's Reasoning in the Trial Scene of Shakespeare's *The Merchant of Venice*

The trial scene in *The Merchant of Venice* has provoked as great a discussion as anything in Shakespeare outside of *Hamlet*. Portia's speech on mercy was the first selection from the English dramatist to be translated into Japanese, and the universal nobility of its sentiments prepared the way for the introduction of his plays into a completely foreign culture. The whole scene has been given mythological overtones by the discovery of its possible relationships to the medieval "Processus Belial" in which the Virgin

---

*The first of these essays was written in response to a request for a short contribution to a *festschrift* for Tauno Mustanoja and was published in a double issue of *Neuphilologische Mitteilungen*, 1–2 78 (1972), Helsinki.

The second represents a last-minute effort to put one little bridge over two large gaps in even this fragmentary study: one, a consideration of legal reasoning as it was actually used; the other, use of the "Secondary Arguments" in that part of logic which the Ramists called "Invention." An adequate investigation of legal logic would require more time and a better knowledge of medieval French and Latin than I have at my disposal.

Mary pleads for mercy against the devil's demand for strict justice toward mankind. German scholars have been fascinated by the relationship of the case against Antonio to the traditions of Roman law, and numerous efforts have been made in various countries to use the scene to bring or refute charges of anti-Semitism against Shakespeare. Since the middle of the nineteenth century a large body of literature, in which this scene plays an important part, has developed in connection with the controversy about Shakespeare's knowledge of and expertise in English law.[1]

Yet critics and scholars appear to have made no attempt to examine Portia's reasoning to discover the logical pattern or patterns which may lie back of it. The difference between the generosity of Portia's plea for mercy and the ruthlessness of her application of the letter of the law to Shylock has often been noted, and Professor George W. Keeton is quite right in saying that the former speech is "so familiar that its deeper significance is in some danger of being overlooked" (*op. cit.*, pp. 142–43). But it does not necessarily follow that its deeper significance may be explained as a layman's prejudice against the rigidity and formality of Common Law and his preference, "following St. Thomas" of Aquinas, for Divine and eternal laws, "both based on perfect reason, and both . . . closely linked with the Law of Nature" (p. 143). In fact, the logical pattern of Portia's reasoning seems to vary. Her first speech was not an appeal to a law based on reason but to reason itself in a logical form distinctively Elizabethan and more closely related to an audience's acute awareness of its own Protestantism rather than of its Catholic heritage. Later she becomes more legalistic, but in two quite different ways.

The logical form was the system of Petrus Ramus, the French Protestant anti-Aristotelian, which required a consideration of eight formal "Arguments" for the primary but full exploration of the logical implications of any matter. These "Arguments" (or "Reasons," as many Ramists called them) were supposed to have a power of persuasion within themselves and might be described in more modern terms as self-evident relationships. These consisted of the absolute or completely "agreeable" relationships of (1) Cause and (2) Effect; the less absolute but still "agreeable" relationship of (3) Subject (something to which something else was attached) and (4) Adjunct or the thing attached (as virtue was attached to its Subject, the soul); "disagreeable" relationships, which might be "differing" in that they were (5) Relative or "somewhat differing" or (6) Opposite because of their disparity or contrariness; and, finally "comparative" relationships of (7) Quantity (equal or, in terms of greater and less, unequal) and (8) Quality (like and unlike). These were the eight "First" Arguments set forth by the Ramists generally and especially by Dudley Fenner in the book which may have been used later by Shakespeare as a guide to the reasoning in Hamlet's soliloquies. Secondary Arguments, growing out of the First, might also be used for the logical "Invention" required to discover the full truth of a matter; and in Fenner's version of the system the most important of these was Testimony, which might be of dubious value if human but was convincing if divine.

Although Portia's first speech covers these "Arguments" or considers these relationships completely, it deviates from Fenner's system at the beginning in two significant ways. In the first place, Portia is led into it by Shylock's query into what the logicians called the "efficient" Cause of mercy. "On what compulsion must I [be merciful]?" he asks. This is a category of causation that Fenner had avoided, and her response, while it fits into the pattern of other Ramists, apparently echoes the language of Thomas Wilson, who in *The Rule of Reason* (1551) had made efficient Causes the first of all and had said: "Some of these causes, worke by

force and violence of nature, some by an outward power,
being streigned thereunto."[2] Portia immediately classifies
the operational Cause of mercy as something which is not
"strained" by external compulsion but which operates by
natural force from within, dropping like "the gentle rain
from heaven." The other deviation from Fenner—and from
the Ramists generally—is in Portia's failure to be explicit
about the formal "Subject" of mercy. The Subject was logically something to which something else was attached,
and Shakespeare clearly thought of mercy as being attached to some form of power. But he was not precise
about the nature of this power and identified it only by
implication throughout Portia's speech. It may be that precision was simply inappropriate to the circumstances (as
was the full analysis of causation), or it may be, as we
shall see later, that Shakespeare was avoiding theological
speculations. Portia's religious sentiments, in any event,
were not allowed to go beyond accepted Protestant doctrine and the explicit Testimony of the Word of God.

In other respects, however, the first fourteen lines (184–
97) of Portia's speech on mercy correspond closely with
Fenner's system of "Arguments." Mercy has the double
Effect of blessing both the giver and the taker. It is an
Adjunct of power but is more becoming to a monarch than
his crown. It is *Relative* or "somewhat differing" from individual to individual, being "mightiest in the mightiest,"
but it is *Disparate* from the temporal power symbolized by
the scepter. In *Quantity* it is superior to and therefore greater
than dread and fear; and in *Quality* it is like something
divine, and unlike earthly power which becomes like God's
only when mercy seasons justice. Throughout the speech
there seems to be an implication that mercy is not only
"an attribute to God himself" but that God may be the
only true *Subject* of that virtue—that is, the one original
source from which it flows. It is this implication which

makes Shakespeare's omission of any formal reference to this "Argument" so teasing. He could have had in mind some Thomistic notions of the identity of Divine and Natural Law. He could have held neo-Platonic notions of human mercy as evidence of divinity in man. Or he could have been implying that man had enough free will to imitate God by being merciful. A clarification of any of these possibilities would involve theological ramifications inappropriate to the theater and uncharacteristic of Shakespeare. All we can be sure of is that Portia's use of the word "quality" at the beginning of her speech gives unusual force to the comparisons with which this section closes.

When Portia turned from primary "Arguments" to the secondary Argument of *Testimony,* however, Shakespeare put her on safe as well as familiar theological grounds. Her next words, "That in the course of justice none of us / Should see salvation," could not be expected to affect the Jew, who, as the more sophisticated members of the audience would know, was under the First Covenant of salvation by strict obedience to the Law. But they could have had a moving effect upon hearers acutely aware (as all Elizabethans were) of their commitment to the Protestant doctrine of Salvation by Grace alone. It was Protestant dogma that this doctrine was supported by the Word of God. Portia's next sentence, "We do pray for mercy, / And that same prayer doth teach us to render / The deeds of mercy," was the most direct possible use that could be made of Divine *Testimony,* for every member of the audience knew that Christ Himself had taught them to pray: "Forgive us our debts, as we also forgive our debters."[3] The allusion was not only appropriate to the situation but to a particular part of the Word of God which was most authoritative and best known to the people.

The thoroughness of her logic and the acuteness of her

religious appeal suggest that Shakespeare's Portia, in this first speech, was less concerned with "this strict court of Venice" than with a potential jury of Englishmen. She made no serious effort to "mitigate the justice" of Shylock's plea, but she did forestall any future appeal he might make either to reason or to Christian charity. One other possibility of appeal remained—one to the principles of English common law, which was based upon precedents. When Shylock falls into her trap by exclaiming, "My deeds upon my head! I crave the law," she closes his last avenue of escape by denying Bassanio's plea that she mitigate the justice of her own decision. "I beseech you," he says, offering to pay the amount of the bond "ten times o'er":

> Wrest once the law to your authority.
> To do a great right, do a little wrong,
> And curb this cruel devil of his will.

"It must not be," she replies:

> 'Twill be recorded for a precedent,
> And many an error, by the same example,
> Will rush into the state. It cannot be.

When Shylock enthusiastically approves of this decision, Portia can go through the formality of giving him another chance to change his mind but she is ready to turn, for the first time, to the law itself.

Portia's concern for the effects caused by a bad precedent is too direct and simple to be attributed to any particular logical pattern, but when she turns to "the law" she abandons the Ramistic exploratory reasoning of her first speech and becomes a strict constructionist of the statutes. The judgment against Antonio, of course, is foreordained, because the facts of the bond are stipulated and Shakespeare's Venetian law, like that of Elizabethan England, fully supported the specified penalty (lines 47–49). Portia's "Tarry a little" for the observation that "The bond doth give thee here no jot of blood" is interpreted by Professor Keeton (pp. 144–45) as a preparation "to move from the realm of Common Law into Equity," but this would be an illogical action to an Elizabethan audience who were well aware (as Professor Keeton elsewhere points out) that suits in Equity were tried in Chancery Courts rather than in Courts of Common Law. In any event, the text does not support this interpretation, for Portia cites another act of statute law, of which Shylock is ignorant, penalizing the shedding of Christian blood. And when Shylock asks in surprise "Is that the law?" she replies, "Thyself shalt see the act."[4]

In the final, climactic part of the court scene Portia is still playing the role of the strict constructionist who becomes a prosecuting judge because she is more learned in the law than are those around her. She brings up still another overlooked statute against the attempt of an alien upon the life of a Venetian citizen and cites it at sufficient length and in sufficient detail to make clear that she is judging the case by the precise letter of the law when she condemns Shylock and turns him over to the mercy of the Duke.

Portia thus appears in three intellectual roles and exemplifies three kinds of reasoning in the trial scene. In her first speech, she is the humane, Christian rationalist, exploring all the logical implications of a subject and relating it to the essence of Protestant doctrine. In her second, when she responds to Bassanio's plea, she is a legal philosopher, reasoning exclusively from cause to consequence and concerned only with the effects of a bad precedent. Finally, when she is acting as a judge, she is a strict constructionist of the statutes, drawing inferences from the letter of the law, judging rigidly when the law covers the case and permitting an appeal for clemency only when the written act provides for it. At the very end, when the Duke is displaying "the difference of our spirits" by his charitable sentence of Shylock, she is careful to protect the rights of Antonio and give him his own chance to show that the quality of mercy, indeed, is not "strained."

From this brief survey of Portia's reasoning it would appear that too much emphasis upon the purely legal aspects of the trial scene limits the critic's view of Shakespeare's purpose and accomplishment. Such legal significance as may exist in the penalty of the "pound of flesh" and in the quibble of "no jot of blood" should be attributed to the Italian sources of the play rather than to Shakespeare's invention, and when Portia is directly concerned with the law she limits herself to the strict and literal interpretation of statutes invented by Shakespeare to serve the purpose of the plot. It is true that these imaginary statutes are based upon principles and couched in terms that make them seem plausible to an English audience generally familiar with the law and its processes, but they do not involve any great legal sophistication.

On the contrary, Portia's reasoning is most impressive and memorable when she is exhibiting Shakespeare's logical rather than legal sophistication. Such sophistication is not always easy to demonstrate in Elizabethan literature because the Ramists differed from other logicians, before and after them, by insisting that "Invention" or the discovery of Arguments was the First Part of Logic which necessarily preceded "Disposition" or the Second Part which dealt with the presentation of Arguments in a persuasive way. As Abraham Fraunce pointed out in *The Lawiers Logike* (one of the most elaborate Ramean treatises of the time) Invention was more appropriate to "solitary meditations and deliberations with a man's self" than to public discourse which had to be directed toward an audience. Portia's speech on mercy is therefore a rare example of discourse in which the pattern of invention is revealed without giving the impression of artificiality and affectation. It represents only a part of her reasoning in the trial scene, but it is the most succinct exhibition in Elizabethan literature of the whole of Ramist "Invention" made evident within a memorable "Distribution" of Arguments that seems universal and unaffected yet had a calculated appeal to the essentials of sixteenth-century Protestantism.

II
The Lawyers Light
on Professional Logic

Most Ramists were concerned with the "Simple" or "Primary" Arguments in their table of "Invention"—Cause and Effect, Subject and Adjunct, Opposites and Comparatives—because they were supposed to have a power of persuasion within themselves insomuch as they discovered and revealed self-evident truth. In the sixteenth century this was probably as true of the lawyer engaged in solitary meditations and deliberations with himself as it was with the theologian searching for the absolute truth of the scriptures, for when Abraham Fraunce revised the manuscript of his textbook for publication as *The Lawiers Logike* he simply added legal illustrations to those derived from Spenser's *The Shepheardes Calendar* without changing his version of the Ramean system. The principal difference between his system and that of the Puritan minister, Dudley Fenner, in fact, was in his elaborate analysis of the idea of causation, which seems to have been of much more importance to lawyers than it was to theologians.

This interest in causation would naturally be greatest in considerations of equity, which was supposed to soften the rigors of common law; but little is known about pleading in the early Chancery courts and nothing at all about the small claims "Courts of Conscience" in which the principles of equity were dominant. A lawyer might approach his case with all the high-mindedness of Shakespeare's Portia in her plea for mercy, but her plea was designed to affect an audience, not a judge, and a full display of her primary reasoning was appropriate to its purpose.

In the actual practice of the law, however, the situation was different. No matter how concerned a lawyer might be with the absolute truth upon which his case might be based, he had to put it before the court in terms of those maxims and precedents which were on record and were therefore a part of that cumulative body of established "law" which guided a judge in his decisions. The professional success of a practicing lawyer, in short, depended upon his ability to find recorded opinions in which his "Primary" Arguments were incorporated or which provided them with acceptable legal support.

The counsellor who was engaged in preparing a case was therefore less concerned with Primary Arguments than with Secondary ones—that is, those which had grown out of the first and had become established as legal principles. These had to be discovered by reading and study, preserved by memory, and used according to a logical arrangement which was dictated by the desire to achieve a favorable judgment. The result was a legal logic within the Ramean pattern which was quite different from that of the person engaged in private meditation or the theologian searching for truth in the scriptures; and the best illustration of it that I have seen is in *The Lawyers Light; Or, A due direction for the study of the Law* by Sir John Doddridge, which was published in 1629, the year of the author's death.[5]

Doddridge was not willing to call himself a Ramist, but,

in *The Lawyers Light*, he used characteristic Ramean terms when he said that in "intending an ample discourse, it shall be requisite to follow the ordinary and best Method, by Definition, Diuision, and the due speculation of their Causes" (p. 2) and when he stressed the importance of "the Art of Logicke" as something "from thence the learned of our Lawes have received many Principles, as well out of that part which concerneth the Inuention of Arguments, as of that which teacheth the disposing, framing the Iudgement of the same" (pp. 7–8). His application of logic to the practice of law was illustrated in the section of his book devoted to what he called *Arbitrements* or judgments made by the court upon cases voluntarily submitted to it for a decision. These cases usually involved principles of equity as well as those of common law with which Doddridge, as a justice of the King's Bench, was primarily concerned. The logic to be used in the preparation of these submissions was succinctly outlined and may be illustrated in the diagram on the following page.

The most significant thing to be observed about this table of Secondary Arguments is that, although it uses some of the same terminology used in identifying Primary Arguments, the words are used within a different frame of reference and therefore with different meanings. An "Argument" is no longer a self-evident truth but becomes a part of the process of persuasion. The "Cause" or moving force of a legal decision was not the reason for making it but the circumstances under which it was made. Of these, to the lawyer preparing his case, the most important or "Efficient" Cause (by which the decision was made) was the judge or judges to whom the controversy was submitted by the parties concerned. It was submitted as the material of a legal action or suit in a form that was rational, purposeful, and clear; and it was finally resolved in a way which ended the controversy by establishing a certainty

which had the "Effect" of law. The performance or enforcement of the decision was an "Adjunct" which might
be added to it but was not necessarily a part of it.

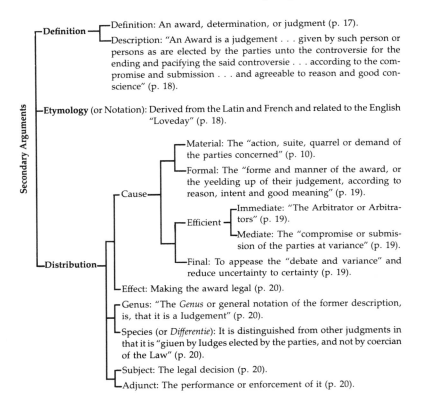

Doddridge denied his Ramism by calling attention to
the fact that he adopted the Aristotelian order in his subdivisions of "Cause" while at the same time pointing out
that those who "affect the Method of *Ramus* . . . begin
with the efficient cause" (p. 32), but he himself explicitly
considered the judge or Arbitrator the Efficient and obviously the most important Cause a lawyer should bear in
mind while preparing his case, devoting more space to a
discussion of it (pp. 26–36) than to all other Causes com-

bined. In other respects, however, he was thoroughly Ramean. The diagram I have made for the visual representation of his systematic treatment of Secondary Causes could be used for practically all English Ramists from Abraham Fraunce to John Milton, although their applications of it were generally less pragmatic and more abstract. Doddridge was an eccentric, and I am not sure how representative he is of legal thinking; but his book suggests that legal logicians made an important contribution to the decay of the Ramean system by placing their emphasis upon Secondary rather than Primary Arguments, by rejecting the Platonism inherent in the same notions of self-evident truth, and by making its terminology less technical and peculiar by bringing it into greater conformity with common usage.

Another suggestion found in Doddridge's book is why the Ramean system continued to be useful in legal reasoning even after the system itself had begun to fall into disrepute. After the forced resignation of Sir Edward Coke, in 1616, as Chief Justice of the King's Bench, the superiority of the chancery court over those of common law was established; and Doddridge, who was one of the justices consulted by Francis Bacon during his assault on Coke's position, may have wanted to preserve in courts of law considerations which would forestall appeals to a supreme court of equity. However this might be, *The Lawyers Light* reveals such a concern. In discussing the duties of a judge he said that they were three: to hear the case, to "judge according to equitie," and to announce the "Award" or decision (p. 29). In a related discussion, later, he said that the rules of common law should be followed with only two exceptions, one based upon equity and the other upon the existence of some contradictory rule of Law, because "for conformities sake" no "absurdity or contradiction" should be permitted "and certain exceptions are framed,

which doe not onely knit and conioyne one Rule in reason
to another, but by meanes of their equitie, temper the
rigour of the Law" (p. 60).

Equity, then, was "no other thing, but an exception of
[i.e., based upon] the Law of God or of Reason from the
generall Rules of the Law of man, when they by reason
of their generality, would in any particular case, iudge
against the Law of God, or the Law of Reason"—"which
exception," he added, is "secretly understood in euery
generall Rule of euery positiue Law" (p. 61). Its importance
was stressed in a summary of the uses of Equity, which
were to keep "the common Law in conformity," to expound
"the Statute Law," and give "remedy in the Court of Conscience in cases of extremitie which otherwise by the Lawes
are leaft undressed" (p. 62). In this allusion to "the Court
of Conscience" Doddridge had obvious reference (made
explicit on p. 65) to the Chancellor's Court which, as he
said, remedied the defects and limited the "ouerlarge letter" of positive law and "giueth likewise comfort, consider-
eth all the circumstances of the fact, and as it were tempered
with the sweetnesse of mercy, and mitigateth the rigour
of the common Law" (p. 64). Nevertheless he was firm in
his defense of the need for what he called positive law.
"All men endewed with the right vse of reason, and con-
uersant in the knowledge of any Law," he insisted, "must
of necessity confesse, that euery Law doth stand vpon
permanent Rules, as of Iron not to be bent or broken vpon
this or that occasion, or to be infringed vpon this or that
occurrence (for else there neede no Court of Law, but all
should be one with the Court of Conscience, and haue
their proceedings framed according to the Arbitrary con-
ceipt of the Iustice)" (p. 62).

Doddridge had based his book upon the assumption
that the law of England had been derived from either "the
Law of Nature" or "some generall Custome vsed within

the Realme" (p. 6), and the problem upon which he tried to focus his lawyer's light was that of achieving justice according to the Law of Nature (or, as he often put it, the Law of Reason) when common or statute law failed to accomplish its just purpose. The legal name for this justice was "equity." It had been traditionally determined by the individual conscience, and the lord "Chancellour, into whose hand the managing thereof within this Realme is committed," was traditionally known as the Keeper of the King's Conscience. But in this age of religious dissent and aggressive sectarianism people had begun to realize that the individual conscience was a vagrant thing—a "wanton spaniel," as men of such different persuasions as Thomas Goodwin and John Dryden were to call it, irresponsibly ready to pursue any triviality. And it may be that such judges as Sir John Doddridge, while bringing the Ramean system of logic down to earth by emphasizing its Secondary Arguments, were willing to use the Primary ones, "secretly understood," as a systematic means for discovering a self-evident truth that would override the letter of the law by considering all circumstances surrounding the facts of a case, tempering it with mercy, and so mitigating its rigor by the higher authority of something generally accepted as "Reason."

Notes

1. The most recent and comprehensive example of this literature is George W. Keeton, *Shakespeare's Legal and Political Background* (London: Sir Isaac Pitman and Sons, 1967), which is the work of a distinguished legal historian who is not only an authority on Elizabethan law but a master of relevant Shakespearean scholarship. I am indebted to him for most of the specific information alluded to above with the exception of the Japanese translation, which was referred to as a matter of common knowl-

edge at a literary conference in Tokyo in 1951 but for which I cannot cite a published source.

2. This quotation, however, is from the 1584 edition, fol. 43r. It may be interesting to note that Wilson is the only authority cited by the OED for the use of the word "strained" in the technical sense that it also appears to have in Portia's opening line.

3. These are the words of the Geneva Bible, Matthew 6:12, which was the most widely read English version in Shakespeare's time. The words "debts" and "debtors" were used in all sixteenth-century English Bibles with the exception of Tyndale's outlawed translation. The word "trespasses" was used in the explanatory verses 14 and 15 which immediately followed the conclusion of the prayer.

4. I am not at all sure, however, that considerations of Equity are entirely missing from the trial scene. My original assumption, in fact, was that Portia's speech on mercy was a calculated attempt to preclude, from the beginning, any appeal to Equity that Shylock might be expected to make. The background for this assumption was no more than an awareness of the parallelism between the extraordinary popularity of Ramean logic in legal circles and the equally extraordinary increase in importance of the Chancery Court during this period. The new logic seems appropriate to the exploration of problems in Equity but not in Common Law, but I have no evidence whatever concerning the actual reasoning used in specific cases in the rival courts.

5. Doddridge's book appeared in two versions: first as *The Lawyers Light*, printed for Benjamin Fisher in 1629, and later as *The English Lawyer* in a much longer version published by the Assignes of J. More, Esq. in 1631. The later publishers claimed that the earlier version was inaccurate and unauthorized. I have used it, however, because of its succinctness and because it is available in a facsimile reprint by the Da Capo Press (New York, 1973). The material I have used in constructing a chart may be found in *The English Lawyer*, pp. 167–70. The author's name is sometimes spelled Doderidge, and *The Lawyers Light* had been falsely attributed to Francis Bacon.

CHAPTER EIGHT

In Justifying
the Ways of God to Men:
The "Invention"
of Milton's
"Great Argument"*

In the Preface to his survey of the system of logic he had acquired at St. Paul's, used at Cambridge, and presumably taught to his nephews John Milton spoke of "art which is a sort of habit of the mind"[1] and implied that he, with others of his school, looked upon logic as the art of arts, underlying and forming all other activities of the intellect. Yet his *Artis logicae* is one of the most neglected of his

---

*This was published, thanks to the open-mindedness of Godfrey Davis, in *The Huntington Library Quarterly* 9 (1) (February 1946). I have had a number of second thoughts about it, the most important of them having reference to pp. 191–93 and especially to the idea of "fortitude to highest victory" as one of the final causes incorporated in man's first disobedience. At the time I wrote I was unaware of the significance of the distinction Milton made between "renovation" and "regeneration" in *De Doctrina Christiana,* Book I, Chapters XVII–XVIII. For most Puritans these terms were interchangeable, but Milton placed an important emphasis upon the "calling" of a natural man to salvation and his consequent "renovation" before he was "regenerated" by a supernatural act of Grace. Because of this I would now be inclined to consider the last two books of *Paradise Lost* (which I treated in a rather cavalier fashion) as a significant survey of the logical natural "end" in Milton's scheme and *Paradise Regained* as a dramatization of the supernatural one.

writings—unfortunately so, for many critical interpretations of his greatest work seem to be made on the basis
of habits of mind quite different from those represented
in the almost forgotten system of his treatise. For example,
Milton's conception of the logical position of Satan in *Paradise Lost* is surely not apparent to those critics who speak
of the author's unconscious satanism; nor can the logic of
Milton's ideas of causation be clear to those who feel that
original sin must be traced back to the motives of "man's
first disobedience." Furthermore, at least some of the curious theological and philosophical implications that have
been recently discovered in the poem disappear when they
are examined with reference to the system of thought which
was a habit of Milton's mind. However valuable the scholarship of Saurat, Tillyard, and—more recently—Maurice
Kelley might be for the light it casts upon the poet's knowledge and ideas, it seems clear that their criticism follows
a way of thinking entirely foreign to that of the seventeenth-century Puritan poet. This alien point of view, I
believe, has introduced into modern criticism problems of
interpretation that did not exist for the "fit audience, though
few," to whom Milton addressed his poem and which should
not exist for the historically-minded readers of today. Thus
it may be worthwhile to direct attention to certain pertinent sections of Milton's relatively unfamiliar work on
logic in an effort to show how these sections might cast
some new—or, rather, old—light on the meaning of *Paradise Lost* and to suggest the effect of his systematic point
of view upon several critical problems that have grown
out of the difference between the mental habits of the poet
and those of his later readers.

The subject is not one, however, which lends itself to
easy clarification even in the oversimplified form of a brief
survey. Accordingly, in treating it, I shall make somewhat
arbitrary divisions dealing with (1) the general character

of Milton's logic and its possible relationship to his statement of his theme and purpose in *Paradise Lost,* with (2) his particular analysis of the logic of causation in his treatise, and with his apparent use of that analysis in *Paradise Lost* in connection with (3) the "efficient" cause, (4) cause as "matter" and "form," and (5) the "final" cause or "end." The contrasts between Milton's logic and that of some of his recent critics will be drawn in the proper sections, although some general comments will be reserved for a brief conclusion.

I

The system of logic offered in Milton's treatise was that of Peter Ramus, amplified in an effort to achieve a "copiousness of clarity" (p. 3) not to be found in the original *Dialecticae libri duo* and modified in several respects in order to conform to Milton's own opinions. The Ramean system, although it was based upon scholastic logic, differed from that of Aristotle in three major ways. Technically, it was an attempt at simplication through the substitution of a fundamental collection of "arguments" for the Aristotelian "predicables" and "categories" or "praedicamenta." Popularly, it placed much more emphasis upon the discovery and statement of axiomatic or self-evident truths than upon careful syllogistic reasoning. And, systematically, it was organized according to a distinctive method of thinking in "dichotomies," moving from the general to the particular by a consistent division of ideas into pairs of mutually exclusive classes until all thought was reduced to its fundamental "arguments." There is no occasion, in this limited paper, to undertake a general discussion of the complete system or of the evidences of Milton's use of it[2] except, perhaps, to point out that its habitual dichotomization is reflected in *Paradise Lost* by Milton's partial definition of "reason" (as he had also defined it in the *Areopagitica*) as "choice" and also, as we shall see, by his limitation of his "argument" through the use of systematic dichotomy in the opening lines of the poem.

In any consideration of the Ramean logic, however, there is some difficulty in terminology, for the Ramists often gave slightly or entirely new meanings to familiar terms borrowed from classical rhetoric and logic. By their method of dichotomy, for example, they divided logic into two parts, "invention" or the seeking out of "arguments," and "disposition" or the arranging of "arguments" in discourse. The second of these included not only the syllogistic arrangements of conventional logic but a great deal of what the Aristotelians considered rhetoric. But the first had almost nothing to do with rhetorical invention. When they spoke of the "invention of arguments" the Ramists meant something like the discovery of self-evident truths rather than the fabrication of persuasive discourse, and, with the Platonic tinge that colored all their thoughts, they thought of "invention" in general as the finding out of something which already existed instead of looking upon it as the putting together of something entirely new. According to their system, "invention" itself was dichotomized, one part leading to the discovery of "artificial" arguments which had the power of proof within themselves and the other to "inartificial" arguments which consisted of either divine or human testimony. The "artificial" part of invention, with which this paper is primarily concerned, was further subdivided into progressively limited classes until it reached "the first of all arguments" which, Milton said, "is *cause*— as any one can know for himself" (p. 29). It was also the argument to which Milton, in common with other Ramists, devoted the most careful attention and analysis, for it was the "first place of invention" and the "fount of all knowledge" (p. 31). Classified according to the amount of space it took up in his textbook, it was certainly the "great" argument in Milton's logical system; and I believe there is evidence worthy of consideration that it (rather than any conventionally heroic narrative or any theological doctrine) was the highest concern and hence the "Great Argument" of the author of *Paradise Lost*.

The poem opens with an identification of its theme by means of a Ramean dichotomy:

Of Man's first disobedience, and the fruit
Of that forbidden Tree, whose mortal taste [the cause]
Brought [the effect] death into the world, and all our woe
With loss of Eden.
[I, 1–4][3]

What Milton wanted illumined in him was his dark vision of the complex nature of that "great argument"—the cause— which was so absolutely coupled with its effect of death and woe and loss of Paradise. He was aware of many "inartificial" arguments related to that effect in the form of divine and human testimony; but although he had a profound faith in divine testimony, having frequently used it as the final argument in his controversial prose writings, the purpose he had set for himself was the discovery of a higher argument which had the power of proof within itself. "When the deepest truth *or nature* of things is carefully sought out," his logic had taught him, "testimony has little force for proof" (p. 281). "And divine testimony," he added, "affirms or denies that a thing is so and brings about that I believe; it does not prove, it does not teach, it does not cause me to know or understand why things are so, unless it also brings forward reasons" (p. 283). Other religious writers had collected testimony and attempted to make it coherent and eloquent. But Milton quite

explicitly thought of himself as pursuing "Things unat-
tempted yet in prose or rhyme." He would use invention,
the first part of logic, to discover the "artificial" argument
that had the power of instructing the rational understanding through its own "innate and peculiar force" (p. 27).
Divine Providence had always been a mystery because of
the inability of corrupted reason to grasp the causes of
God's ways to men.[4] Milton's bold purpose was literally
to "assert"—to join himself to—Eternal Providence in a
logical effort to make the ways of God to men (to the extent
of this one particular "argument") as right and clear to
human reason as Providence itself might make them to
uncorrupted faith.

II

The richness of invention demanded by Milton's purpose may be realized when one remembers that the Ramean "argument" is not a matter of mere words or even
things[5] but something which has within itself "a natural
bent" for "showing, explaining, or proving" its subject matter (pp. 23–25). It is something which served in the Ramean
system of logic as a substitute for the Aristotelian predi-
cable and category without representing either the relationship of the former or the abstract concept of the latter.
It bears some resemblance to the category but has a closer
(although—to the un-Platonic mind, at least—tenuous and
difficult) connection with the thing itself. Cause could be
stated, for example, by definition as Milton defined the
cause of death and all our woe as "Man's first disobedience" in the opening line of *Paradise Lost*. But such a definition was "nothing else than a universal symbol of the
causes constituting the essence and nature of a thing" (p.
265). In order to bring out the full power of this "argument"

Milton had to examine, with some precision, the thing itself and distinguish all the varied causes that constituted the nature and essence of original sin and present them in a way that would reveal their "natural bent for showing, explaining, or proving" it. The Ramean method of invention was that of elaborate "distribution" into classes and subclasses of cause by the process of dichotomy, and the distribution of this "first of all arguments" provided most of the subject matter of the poem.

The system of logic provided by Milton's treatise, however, was not fully equal to the task laid upon it; and Milton, by the time he wrote *Paradise Lost,* may have been willing to permit himself some satiric reference to the academic subtleties of formal logic in his portrait of the rhetorically impassioned Satan with the power

> not only to discern
> Things in their causes, but to trace the ways
> Of highest agents, deemed however wise.   [IX, 681–83]

But the "habit of the mind" remained, and his invention followed the academic pattern although some evidences of it, especially when the system itself broke down, may be debatable. The first distributions of "cause" are clear: it was dichotomized into two nameless genera which were in turn respectively divided into "efficient" and "matter," "form" and "end." These resembled the Aristotelian classifications from which the Ramists borrowed the descriptive names without, however, adopting their exact Aristotelian signification. For one thing, the strong Platonic bias of the Ramists made their conception of "matter" somewhat more intangible than the Aristotelian "material" cause; and, for another, their conception of the "efficient" cause would not allow it to fit into any discoverable genus.[6] Indeed, the Ramean conception of the efficient cause was

so complex (of such "richness," as Milton put it [p. 33])
that with it the whole system of distribution broke down.
But Milton's attempt to deal with it takes up three entire
chapters in the *Artis logicae* and forms an essential key to
his thinking in *Paradise Lost*.

The distinctive peculiarity of Milton's treatment of the
efficient cause is that, for reasons we shall notice later, he
did not consider it a single cause or even a consecutive
series of causes. The efficient, like the more general concept of cause, was subject to analysis or distribution into
parallel causes which were independent of each other so
far as the human mind could perceive. It was here that
the Ramean system, as Milton developed it somewhat far-
ther than most of his predecessors, failed; for there was,
he admitted, no apparent possibility of dividing the efficient cause into mutually exclusive species according to
the proper method of dichotomy. Accordingly he explored
its richness through three classical "modes of working"
which were dichotomized as "procreative and maintaining," "singly and with others," and "by itself and by its
accidence." All three appear in *Paradise Lost*, but the second
is by far the most important in the poem and is also the
one most carefully analyzed in the *Artis logicae*. The "other"
causes in this mode of working (that is, those with which
the efficient operates) were represented as being either
"principal" or "helping," and the "helping" causes were
further classified as either "impulsive" or "instrumental."
The "impulsive" cause, which "in some way" impelled or
moved the "principal," was itself distributed into a "proegumenic" cause (which moved from within the principal)
and a "procatarctic" (which moved or operated from without); and, finally, the latter represented either the genuine
"occasion" or a feigned "pretext." Beginning students of
Ramean logic were not expected to keep all such classifications within classification in their minds, and one of the

distinctive features of most Ramean textbooks was something that might be described as a sort of table of logical logarithms. Milton's analysis of the efficient cause, diagrammed as a continuation of the conventional Ramean table, would appear as the accompanying diagram. To discover all "the causes constituting the essence and nature" of man's original sin it will be necessary to consider all the terminal words of this table; and such a consideration, I believe, will account for the greater part of the "invention" in *Paradise Lost*.

During the course of this consideration, however, two things must be constantly borne in mind. One is that, to Milton, "invention" and "disposition" were two entirely separate divisions of the art of logic, and the discovery of arguments had no relation to the disposition of them according to the epic plan of discourse. The other—and more tenuous one—is that Milton was unable to name the genus in which the efficient cause was placed. This means that the unconscious tendency to think of the natural order of causes in terms of *time* must be consciously overcome: the "efficient," in particular, did not in all its manifestations necessarily pre-exist matter, nor do the various subdivisions of the efficient cause bear any necessary temporal relationship to other causes in the table.

With these things in mind, then, and with constant reference to his logical table, let us observe Milton's representation of "the causes constituting the essence and nature" of the original sin which "Brought death into the world, and all our woe."

III

"The efficient is the beginning of motion and the first of causes," Milton wrote in the *Artis logicae* (p. 57); and he

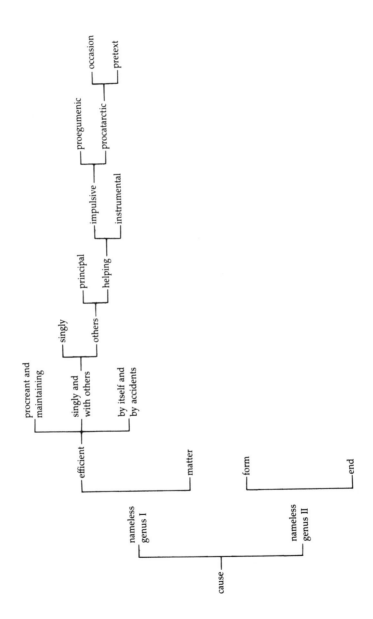

properly began *Paradise Lost* with a statement of the first cause, which, to adapt his own figure of speech, was the beginning of motion in the womb of chaos. One crucial point about his habit of thinking, however, was that he thought of the "first" efficient cause as not only operating *through* other causes but *with* other causes which, though of a lower order, were themselves efficient. In other words, his system of logic provided for independent or parallel efficient causes which were not derived from some "first cause" in any way perceptible to the human mind. These parallel causes were certainly not looked upon as links in some necessary chain of causation, for the conclusion to the chapter from which the tabular analysis is taken refers to a chain of causes as something in addition to the classification:

> To this place it seems may be assigned most conveniently the order of causes in which one is called *first*, either absolutely, as God, or in its genus, as the sun and anything of the sort; others, called *secondary* and so forth depend on the first or the prior causes, and each is a kind of effect [pp. 37–39].

"But," he added,

> these divisions in the causes of logic need not be zealously followed out, for the whole force of arguing is contained in the proximate cause; and from this alone the general definition of cause is understood [p. 39].

Milton did not deny a chain of causation. He simply ignored it as an unfathomable mystery that had no place in the human art of logic which involved "the actual teaching of something useful" (p. 13); and it had no part in the invention of *Paradise Lost*.[7]

Milton, in fact, allowed God to disassociate himself entirely from the other "more proximate" efficient causes which contained "the whole force" of proving, teaching, or causing one to "know or understand why things are so":

> So without least impulse or shadow of fate,
> Or aught by me immutably forseen,
> They trespass, authors to themselves in all,
> Both what they judge and what they choose. [III, 120–23]

Man, in the person of Adam, was the "principal" cause of his own first disobedience. But even though he was the "principal" he was affected by certain explicable impulses and by an instrument of deception which could be classified as "helping" causes. The "instrumental cause" was of particular importance because it enabled divine justice to draw a distinction between the fate of man's fellow sinners—the fallen angels—and his own:

> The first sort by their own suggestion fell,
> Self-tempted, self-depraved; Man falls, deceived
> By the other first: Man therefore shall find grace;
> The other none.   [III, 129–32]

So important was this instrumental cause to the clarification of God's ways to men that Milton turned immediately to it at the beginning of his poem, appealing to the Holy Spirit to

>   say first what cause
> Moved our grand parents, in that happy state,
> Favoured of Heaven so highly, to fall off
> From their Creator.   [I, 28–31]

Satan, "the infernal Serpent," he declares at once was the seducer of mankind—the instrument of man's "foul revolt." But such a simple statement is not a true "artificial" argument because it does not have "a natural bent for showing, explaining, or proving" anything in itself. Satan must be considered in all his pride and subtlety, as the adventurous spirit and master politician that he was, in order to become a convincing argument according to the demands of Milton's particular system of logic. The presentation of Satan in his logical character is a work of great art, and it reflects a considerable amount of that dramatic sympathy—the ability of the artist to identify himself momentarily with his subject—which may be a characteristic of all convincing writers. But it does not reflect, as so many critics since William Blake have assumed, any "unconscious" sympathy between the author and his creation or indicate that "unwittingly he was led away by the creature of his imagination."[8] The Milton who so explicitly maintained that "art is not commonly against the will . . . and the prudent and well informed man makes use of thought" (p. 41) would hardly have composed so great a part of his artistic masterpiece against his expressed will or without taking adequate thought of what he was doing. On the contrary, "the art of reasoning well"[9] demanded that the instrumental cause of the world's great catastrophe should be sufficiently impressive to have the power of "showing, explaining, or proving" its part in that catastrophe by its own "innate and peculiar force." Had Milton's hatred of evil made him represent Satan, up to the time of the fall, as a mean and contemptible figure he actually would have been led away from his logical habits of mind by the creature of his imagination. That he did not do so merely shows that his logical habits were different from those of his later critics.

The bare statement that man was the "principal" cause of his first disobedience—like the identification of Satan as the instrument of his fall—is an inadequate "artificial" argument because it does not have the power of "showing,

explaining, or proving" within itself. To give his argument
that power it was necessary for Milton to characterize Adam
as fully as he characterized Satan, though from a somewhat different point of view because in Adam he had to
discover the "proegumenic" cause which, although strictly
an impulsive "helping" cause, somehow moved the principal from within. God had made Adam

>   just and right,
> Sufficient to have stood, though free to fall;   [III, 98–99]

and in this freedom lay the chief difference between man
and the Creator in whose image he had been formed.
Adam himself identified it through his own self-knowl-
edge as a "deficience" (VIII, 416) in his nature and was
praised by God for recognizing it (VIII, 437 ff.). Briefly, it
was an inability to be satisfied by himself, a lack of self-
sufficiency as Tillyard has aptly called it, which was

>   The cause of his desire
> By conversation with his like to help
> Or solace his defects.   [VIII, 417–19]

It was this lack of self-sufficiency, this need for companionship, which led to the creation of Eve, who, in turn,
provided the "procatarctic" cause (operating from without)
or "occasion" for the fall. Having sinned herself, she provided Adam with the occasion to choose between his "happy
state" and the companionship of his "other self," testing
his

>   unity defective; which requires
> Collateral love, and dearest amity.   [VIII, 425–26]

Adam's unexercised reason was not proof against the requirements of his "unity defective," and so the "deficience"

of his nature operated from within as an impulsive cause that brought about his sin,

> Against his better knowledge, not deceived,
> But fondly overcome with female charm.   [IX, 998–99]

This summary analysis of the operation of the efficient cause in the major argument of *Paradise Lost* is by no means complete, but it should be sufficient to show that each of the characters in the drama of man's first disobedience occupies a role designed by Milton's conception of that cause as set forth in his *Art of Logic*. God is the remote first cause, who moves in so mysterious a way that human reason can find a force for teaching only in those more proximate causes with which he works. Adam, impelled by a "deficience" of nature within him, was the principal cause of "all our woe." Eve provided the occasion of his first disobedience. And Satan was the instrument by which the catastrophe was brought about. The next two causes that combined with the efficient and final causes to form the "great argument" may be more briefly treated.

IV

In the classification of causes which Milton adopted for his system of logic, "matter" was placed with the "efficient" in the first of two nameless genera into which causes were dichotomized. The two belonged together even though there was no resemblance between them that would enable the logician to name the genus, for they complemented each other in a way that affected Milton's entire characterization of Adam before the fall. Satan introduced this new element in the invention of Milton's "great argument" with his proposal to explore the "matter" of God's new

creation, "the cause from which" (p. 51) man's first disobedience came:

> Thither let us bend all our thoughts, to learn
> What creatures there inhabit, of what mould,
> Or substance, how endued, and what their power,
> And where their weakness.   [II, 354–57]

Carrying out his proposal, he found on earth the newly
created man, molded of the dust in God's image and in-
dued with the knowledge of himself and of all the world
in which he lived. This knowledge was natural reason,
and with it went free will and the power to choose good
or evil. His knowledge was perfect so far as it went, but,
being of a world and of a creature free from sin, it was
incomplete. Adam had no direct knowledge of good and
evil. The fruit of that tree had been kept from him as a
test of his obedience, but to make any disobedience on his
part "inexcusable" (V, Argument) he had been allowed the
best indirect knowledge possible to him: the testimony of
Raphael, who told him of the revolt in heaven and of the
nature of the evil which threatened him. To Milton, however, who believed that "when the deepest truth or nature
of things is carefully sought out, testimony has little force
for proof," Adam's innocence was the "matter," one of the
causes, from which original sin came. It was the passive
complement of the impulsive cause of Adam's sin.

The failure to consider "matter" as a formal cause in the
argument of *Paradise Lost* is another illustration of the difference between the habits of thinking exhibited by the
recent critics and the author of the poem. Tillyard's troubled efforts to explain the "mental levity" of Adam and
Eve as an active "motive"—a sort of efficient cause—leading up to the fall,[10] for example, is a result of that difference.
By summarizing Milton's attitude in such phrases as "Eve's

resistance was inexcusably trivial" and "Adam reaches the height of criminal levity" and by finding in *Paradise Lost* the same scornful attitude toward "levity and shallowness of mind" that was expressed in *The Tenure of Kings and Magistrates*, he succeeds in giving the impression (to an uncharitable reader, perhaps) that Milton felt he would have done a little bit better than Adam had he been the first man. He does not bear in mind, as Milton undoubtedly did, that before the fall Adam was different in "matter" from mankind afterwards. His "levity and shallowness of mind" was the product of innocence; that of Milton's contemporaries was not and therefore, unlike Adam's, could properly be attributed to a "numb and chill stupidity of soul." There may be a certain amount of "grim humor" in Milton's treatment of his "great grand parents," but there is no suggestion of smugness or of the contempt and scorn that he poured out upon the later and relatively minor sinners he dealt with in his prose works. He could not praise a fugitive and cloistered virtue, but the virtue of an innocence so complete that it would not even flee from evil was the matter of tragedy rather than of contempt.

The third of the major subdivisons under which Milton treated the argument of "cause," hardly lent itself to the sort of elaborate descriptive presentation that the others invited. Milton defined "form" as "the cause through which a thing is what it is" or that "which gives the peculiar essence of the thing." A Platonic conception of something which "is produced in the thing simultaneously with the thing itself," it could be illustrated concretely only through its effect. The "form" of man's first disobedience was the change in the nature of man that accompanied original sin and made it the terrible catastrophe which it was. Described through its effects, it was the change of the innocent imperfections of human nature into sinful passions as appetite became intemperance and the companionship of wedded love became lustful intercourse. "Their Maker's image," as Michael put it, "forsook them" (XI, 515–16), and right reason was corrupted. With this change in the nature of man, sin and death took up their dwelling in the world and even physical nature lost its benignant character. Man and, incidentally, his environment were henceforth to be different in essence from what they had been before.

Yet, in this case again, a failure to recognize the importance of "form" as the "cause through which a thing is what it is" has resulted in the critical implication of sin in Eden before the fall occurs. The persistent feeling of some critics that Adam's sin must be something more deadly, or more conventionally sinful, than the mere act of disobedience appears to be influenced in part at least by their unawareness of that cause which gives a "peculiar essence" to acts that are otherwise innocent.[11] Saurat, for example, although he carefully refers to "sensuality" as a "consequence" of the fall and discusses Milton's conception of "legitimate sensuality,"[12] nevertheless refers to the forbidden fruit as "an aphrodisiac" thus implying that the effects of the fall were merely to amplify an evil inherent in human nature from the creation.[13] Tillyard, while denying that Adam's sin is sensuality,[14] is even more explicit in pushing original sin back to some point before the fall, linking it to the active motive of "levity" which is apparently considered inherent in human nature, especially feminine nature. "Eve's prime sin," he finally decides, "is a dreadful unawareness, despite all warnings, of the enormous issues involved"—that is, her sin is simply her prelapsarian innocence.[15] Adam's "final sin," he also concludes, is "uxoriousness," which also became evident before the fall. Now there is no doubt that Milton represented Eve as possessing sensual appetite and Adam as being susceptible to female charms (which might be interpreted as either passion or uxoriousness), but there is no indication that he considered the first sinful in itself or that he looked upon the second as anything more than a natural concomitant to the innocent "deficience" in human nature which distinguished man from God. The "form" of sin, entering into them, gave them the peculiar essence which Milton condemned in his descriptions of the intemperance of appetite and lust after the fall. Both Saurat and Tillyard apparently fell into the logical trap of thinking not in terms of Milton's classification of parallel causes but in terms of a non-Miltonic chain of causation that inevitably makes the "original sin" of Adam the effect of some earlier sin or sinful motive.

V

The final cause or "end" ("the cause for the sake of which a thing is") has received an excessive amount of attention from critics of *Paradise Lost*—especially in view of the fact that Milton actually rather neglected it in that poem, indicating it through the conversation of Adam and Michael instead of developing it fully as an "argument" with its own innate and peculiar force. The clearest indication he gave of the "end" of man's first disobedience was the conventional one: only after man's sin and the introduction of death into the world could God exhibit his surpassing love through the sacrifice of the Mediator or his infinite mercy by allowing some human beings to achieve a "far happier place" than the Paradise of Eden. In the customary phrase, so popular among the Puritans, the final cause of the fall was "the greater glory of God." Adam understood this when he exclaimed:

O Goodness infinite, Goodness immense!
That all this good of evil shall produce,

And evil turn to good; more wonderful
Then that by which creation first brought forth
Light out of darkness! Full of doubt I stand,
Whether I should repent me now of sin
By me done and occasioned, or rejoice
Much more, that much good thereof shall spring,
To God more glory, more good will to men
From God, and over wrath grace shall abound.

[XII, 469–78]

But Milton also indicated a more proximate and less conventional end. This was the

       argument
Not less but more heroic than the wrath
Of stern Achilles . . .
. . . the better fortitude
Of patience and heroic martyrdom   [IX, 13–32]

which Adam suffered and many good men, following Christ,
were to suffer in the future. This, as Adam realized, was
"fortitude to highest victory" (XII, 570), the greatest
achievement possible to man and one which was infinitely
greater than any that would have been possible to him in
his happy state of innocence. To Milton, a great humanist
as well as a Puritan, the end of the fall was not only the
greater glory of God but the greater glory of man; and the
realization of that was the sum of highest wisdom. But
there were in Adam's history no incidents of patience and
heroic martyrdom sufficiently dramatic to have within
themselves a "natural bent for showing, explaining, or
proving" the heroic nature of that part of his "argument."
The full exploration of the richness of invention contained
in the final cause could not be made through Adam: it
required the history of that "greater man" whose fortitude
of patience and heroic martyrdom bore witness, at once,

to the glory of man and of God. The "invention" of Milton's "great argument" was not complete until his logic called *Paradise Regained* out of the well of his imagination.[16]

The tendency of critics to place an undue stress upon the final cause or "end" in *Paradise Lost* has involved them in a Laocoönian struggle with theological problems that are relatively unimportant in the poem. Following Pope's reading of Milton's purpose as an attempt to "vindicate" or defend God's behavior toward mankind—to show the good rather than all the reasons or causes in it—these critics have shown an excessive concern over the theology of *Paradise Lost,* and one of the most recent of them has implied by the title of his study that the "great argument" of the poem is entirely a theological one.[17] That Milton composed his poem generally in accord with the theological beliefs he was trying to systematize in *De doctrina Christiana* is of course true, but it does not necessarily follow either that *Paradise Lost* was supposed to reflect the systematic theology of the treatise or that the "dogma, aims, and argument"[18] of the poem are in any sense parallel terms. Such mooted questions as Milton's Arianism or Arminianism, in fact, seem entirely irrelevant to the interpretation of *Paradise Lost.* There God appears as a remote first cause. Christ, in one manifestation, is the instrumental cause of the creation and, in another, is a final cause of man's disobedience. Milton's treatment of each is restricted by the logical demands of an argument which has nothing at all to do with the theological problem of explaining the nature of their being and their relationship. There may not be much doubt concerning Milton's Arianism, but it is difficult to see how a strict Trinitarian who accepted the Ramean system of logic could have found grounds for protest against his treatment of the Father or the Son in his poem.

The fact seems to be that the heterodoxies of *Paradise*

Lost are relatively modern discoveries made by readers whose habits of mind are quite different from Milton's. His contemporaries were surely sensitive to theological differences, but the accounts of his contemporary reputation have recorded no complaints at the lack of orthodoxy in his poem.[19] The Arminian controversy was certainly alive in America during the late seventeenth and early eighteenth centuries when strict Calvinists studied the *Artis logicae* in Harvard College and read *Paradise Lost* without the slightest disturbances to their theological sensitivities.[20] Indeed, the whole question of Milton's Arminianism, in *Paradise Lost* and in *De doctrina Christiana*, should be reviewed once more against the background of his system of logic.[21] To persons with a habit of thinking about efficient causes as a series of causal phenomena, the concept of human free will is a broken link in the chain of causation and a denial of the efficiency of the first cause. But this was not the habit of Milton, who dichotomized the "efficient" into causes which were parallel rather than linked in series and dismissed the "order of causes" from first to second and so forth as something which "need not be zealously followed out." Thus when he wrote,

> Man shall not quite be lost, but saved who will;
> Yet not of will in him, but grace in me
> Freely voutsafed,   [III, 173–75]

he was not giving expression to an Arminian theological doctrine[22] so much as he was stating his habitual dichotomization of the efficient cause: man's will is the impulsive helping cause of his salvation, God's grace the instrumental cause. Both were efficient. The order of causes connecting man's will with God's was simply ignored as being beyond the realm of those proximate causes which contained "the whole force of arguing." The ambiguity of

God's expression of willingness to lend an ear and eye to "prayer, repentance, and obedience due" (III, 191) may be indicative of Milton's Arminian leanings. But it may indicate nothing more than a desire to avoid controversial theology, and a strict Calvinist who was also a thoroughgoing Ramist would have found this section of *Paradise Lost* quite tolerable. One reason for the great popularity of the Ramean logic among the Puritans was possibly the ease with which it permitted a superficial reconciliation between the doctrines of moral agency and predestination, and the somewhat incidental theology of *Paradise Lost* appears to reflect this reconciliation rather than a clear-cut Arminian heterodoxy.

One further illustration may emphasize the importance of Milton's system of logic to a thorough understanding of *Paradise Lost:* Saurat discusses the doctrine of "retraction" expressed in the following lines,

> I uncircumscribed myself retire,
> And put not forth my goodness, which is free
> To act or not,   [VII, 170–72]

as "the very centre of his metaphysics";[23] and Tillyard is inclined "to think that Saurat is right in stressing them and in *reading into them* as much as he does" because he himself has "*felt* the 'retraction' of God from Paradise, the gradual freeing of the wills of Adam and Eve till by the time of uttermost trial the process is complete."[24] Both critics comment upon this doctrine as an example of Milton's highly unconventional thinking, and the former goes so far as to speak of it as one of the "peculiar conceptions . . . found nowhere else" than in the *Zohar* although he suspects that it might occur somewhere in the writings of Robert Fludd.[25] Now the particular passage quoted may have been derived from the sources Saurat suggests, but that would not mean that the

Zohar provided anything more than a convenient ontological illustration of "conceptions" that existed as a sort of habit of Milton's mind long before he engaged in any of the esoteric reading that Saurat assumes. For the "retraction" which Tillyard "felt" throughout the poem and which caused the French critic to read into a few lines as much as he did was not in the least bit unconventional during Milton's time. On the contrary, it is the very essence of his Ramean treatment of the "efficient cause" which, by practically ignoring the chain of causation beginning with the "first," in effect "retracted" God from consideration in dealing with those "proximate" causes that argue "with the greatest strength" (p. 53) and so are most important in instructing the human mind.[26] Indeed, the conception of this sort of "retraction" was so widespread among the Puritans of Milton's generation that a group of Puritan clergymen in England and Ireland undertook to counteract it by collecting an overwhelming number of instances that had an innate and peculiar power for arguing the immediacy of God as an efficient cause in human affairs. Had it not been for the effect of the Restoration upon the fortunes of its undertakers, the project might have been published as a Puritan monument entirely different from *Paradise Lost* though contemporaneous with it. Circumstances, however, dictated that Master Samuel Hartlib should transfer it to America, and *An Essay for the Recording of Illustrious Providences* is remembered as an aberration of Increase Mather rather than as a document of the English Puritanism which designed it to counteract the widespread concern for more "proximate" causes.

VI

Milton and his fellow Puritans were not simple people, but one may be permitted to doubt whether they were quite so complicated as some modern students of "the Puritan mind" and of Milton's writings would have us believe. Attempts to systematize their expressions of opinion according to modern habits of thinking have resulted in such complications that, in one notable instance, Thomas Shepard is represented as maintaining as a means of salvation a doctrine which he specifically denounced as an easy way to hell;[27] and some Milton scholars give the impression that they look upon *Paradise Lost* as a sort of "Kubla Khan" in which the author allows his subconsciousness to run riot while he preaches theology and lets the Lord make double-talk. When one sees *Paradise Lost* crumble into intellectual incoherence at the hands of Milton's critics and then re-reads the poem, he is forced to consider the probability that somewhere the poet and his interpreters have parted company—that the words written in the seventeenth century no longer mean the same thing when they are read in the twentieth. The discovery of similar divergences between other Puritans and their most careful readers suggests, furthermore, that the parting has been so general that the point of separation must be sought outside the limits of that field of intellectual history which these same scholars are so earnestly—and, I am afraid, at times so fruitlessly—exploring. It seems impossible, in short, to make sense of the opinions of the seventeenth-century Puritans without taking into greater consideration the logical matrix in which these opinions were formed.

The history of logic has not been written with reference to its practical effect upon human thought, but when such a history is written I suspect it will place more emphasis upon what Milton called "invention" than upon the "disposition" of the reasoning processes with which professional logicians seem primarily concerned. If that should be so, I suspect, further, that the habits of thinking about causes will receive the attention they deserve and the En-

glish-speaking Puritans will be seen in their proper per-
spective. Believing in an efficient cause that might work
by itself or with others, they lived in a world in which God
might interfere directly with human affairs or retract himself in order that more proximate causes might operate;
and, accepting that world, they had a double duty of un-
questioning obedience to Divine Providence and unceas-
ing effort to discover all the proximate causes that had any
power for teaching. There was straight Ramean logic in
the reputed command to trust in God and keep your powder dry, for no one could know how the efficient cause
might choose to work its effect in any particular case. They
could look with equal favor upon Milton's attempt to make
the ways of God to men comprehensible at the level of the
highest mystery and upon Increase Mather's effort to make
them mysterious on the lowest plane of everyday life. The
chance of mystery and the possibility comprehension always existed side by side, and no man could tell without
investigation whether he was supposed to abide in ignorance or reach an understanding. Their way of thinking
about the efficient cause in this mode of operation is no
longer ours, and I also suspect that a history of logic in
its practical effects would show that our way of thinking
parted from the Puritan way when the scientific movement, in itself and in its impact upon a religious people,
reinvigorated the chain of causation as a habit of thought.
After Newton, Englishmen developed an increasing tendency to prove the existence of God by reference to a series
of effects, and the habits of investigation that the Puritans
themselves encouraged eventually deadened men's interest in the mystery. John Milton was modern enough in
the direction his mind took in *Paradise Lost:* the greatest
difficulty in understanding him, I believe, is the difficulty
of following him in that direction along a logical path that

has been so completely abandoned and so nearly forgotten.

The Ramean conception of logic as "the art of disputing well" makes a rediscovery of the path, in any paticular case, uncertain; and Milton's logic often differs with that of other Ramists, and in its complexities and second thoughts it is not always thoroughly consistent with itself.[28] Such uncertainty and inconsistency—in the present state of our knowledge—make an entirely satisfactory survey of the logical invention in *Paradise Lost* impossible. But a preliminary essay in that direction should suggest that the poem is more rationally coherent than certain modern trends in critical scholarship would have us believe. It was not Milton but his later critics who made illogical the ways of God to men.

Notes

1. *A Fuller Institution of the Art of Logic, Arranged after the Method of Peter Ramus, by John Milton, an Englishman* (trans. A. S. Gilbert, *The Works of John Milton*, XI [New York: The Columbia University Press, 1935]), 9. Further references to this edition will be made by page number within the text.

The earliest known edition of the original Latin text of the *Artis logicae* was published in London, 1672, although it may have appeared earlier. There have been a number of rather casual speculations concerning the date of composition, the most plausible being that it grew out of notes made at Cambridge and systematized during Milton's own period of teaching with perhaps some revision just before publication. See John W. McCain, Jr., "Milton's 'Artis Logicae'" and "Further Notes on Milton's 'Artis Logicae,'" *Notes and Queries* 154 (March 4, 1933): 149, and 155 (July 29, 1933): 56, for some comments upon its background and publication. G. C. Moore Smith, "A Note on Milton's 'Art of Logic,'" *Review of English Studies* 13 (July 1937): 335, makes additional comments upon its origin and suggests certain parallels between it and *Paradise Lost*.

2. Franklin Irwin, *Ramistic Logic in Milton's Prose* (unpublished dissertation, Princeton, 1941) has illustrated Milton's dependence upon this system of logic in the prose pamphlets of the 1640s and in the treatise on Christian doctrine.

3. All quotations from *Paradise Lost* are by book and line from the edition by A. W. Verity (Cambridge, 1921).

4. *"Ignorance of causes has fabricated the name of fortune,"* he wrote in the *Artis logicae;* and "certainly fortune should be placed in heaven, but should be called by the different name of *divine providence"* (p. 49).

5. "An argument in the proper sense of the word is not a word or a thing, but a certain fitness of something for arguing" (p. 25).

6. For example, the "efficient" cause was both "intrinsic" (with "matter" and "form") and "extrinsic" (with "end"); and, in time, it both preceded and followed "matter" and could be coexistent with the "end."

7. The efficient "first" cause (i.e., God) in its "procreant and maintaining" mode has an important subordinate place in the invention of the poem, and the difference between its operation by itself and by its accidence is also important to a complete logical analysis. But this discussion seems complicated enough without introducing these overlapping "modes of working" although they are highly significant with reference to Milton's religious beliefs.

8. See E. M. W. Tillyard, *Milton* (London, 1934), 277 in his chapter "Paradise Lost: the Unconscious Meaning." I cite Tillyard's as the most nearly reasonable of all the expositions of this point of view, for although he adopts it he avoids the extremes of what he calls the "purely Satanic explanations."

9. It might be noted in passing that Milton's definition of logic (p. 19) differs somewhat from the more conventional Ramean *Dialectica est ars bene disserendi.*

10. E. M. W. Tillyard, *Milton,* 260–66 passim.

11. This is not by any means true of all critics. Edwin Greenlaw, "A Better Teacher than Aquinas," *Studies in Philology* 14 (April 1917): 196, identifies Adam's sin as passion or intemperance without implying its sinfulness before it took the form of disobedience. And, in general, H. J. C. Grierson, *Milton and Words-*

worth (Cambridge, 1937), is consistently sensitive and discriminating in avoiding logical implications that do not exist in *Paradise Lost.*

12. Denis Saurat, *Milton: Man and Thinker* (New York, 1925), 152, 155 ff.

13. Ibid. 152. Cf. his discussion of Eve, 160 and passim. Saurat's conception of Milton as a "pantheistic deist," in fact, makes it practically impossible for him to look upon the fall as representing *original* sin.

14. E. M. W. Tillyard, *Milton,* 262.

15. Ibid. 261. According to this interpretation, Eve's sin was her failure to possess a thorough knowledge of good and evil, and thus the eating of the forbidden fruit should not have been a sin at all but an act that made it possible for man to avoid sin. If Tillyard had developed the full implications of this interpretation, he would have had mankind acquiring rather than losing free will through his first disobedience.

16. As a logician Milton held that "there is no true distribution" of the final cause although there are "distinctions of special ends" some of which can be subordinate to the highest (p. 69); and he would have admitted, had he not been able to illustrate them both in one person, that the "greater glory of man" was merely a subordinate end. His emphasis upon the humanity of Christ in *Paradise Regained* may have been the result of his belief that the more proximate cause had the greater force for teaching. The examination of Milton's logic, in general, strengthens the view of him as a practical man who lacked the refined, almost mystical piety which characterized such a Cambridge contemporary, for example, as Thomas Shepard.

17. Maurice Kelley, *This Great Argument: A Study of Milton's De Doctrina Christina as a Gloss upon* Paradise Lost (Princeton, 1941).

18. Ibid. ix.

19. See Raymond D. Havens, "Seventeenth Century Notices of Milton" and "The Early Reputation of *Paradise Lost,*" *Englishe Studien* 40 (1909): 175, 187; and William R. Parker, *Milton's Contemporary Reputation* (Columbus, Ohio, 1940).

20. In all the material upon which I have commented in two articles, "Early American Copies of Milton," *The Huntington Library Bulletin* 7 (April 1935): 169 and "The Influence of Milton

on Colonial American Poetry," *The Huntington Library Bulletin* 9 (April 1936): 63, I have found no signs of any interest in the theological implications of *Paradise Lost*.

21. Franklin Irwin, in the dissertation cited, has attempted to study this treatise in the light of Milton's logic; but his failure to devote careful attention to Milton's distribution of the efficient cause in its mode of working "with others" and his inability to refrain from naming the genera which Milton declared "nameless" have, it seems to me, vitiated his analysis.

22. Kelley, *This Great Argument*, 15, quotes these lines as evidence that Milton did not hold to the Calvinistic theory of predestination at the time *Paradise Lost* was written.

23. Saurat, *Milton: Man and Thinker*, 124 and passim.

24. E. M. W. Tillyard, *Milton*, 274. The italics are my own.

25. Saurat, 298, 302n.

26. Despite Milton's rather melancholy appeal for a "fit audience . . . though few," the importance of his desire to teach can hardly be over-emphasized. Cf. *Artis logicae:* "The form of an art . . . [is] . . . the actual teaching of something useful" (p. 13). "All agree, besides, that what is taught should be useful in the life of men . . . and that anything is unworthy the name of art which does not make its aim something good or useful for human life, and honorable as well" (pp. 13–15).

27. At least I do not believe that I am doing an injustice to Perry Miller who, in the special bibliography for his chapter on "The Covenant of Grace" in *The New England Mind* (New York, 1939), lists Thomas Shepard's *The Sincere Convert* as one of the particularly "important" works through which the "idea and philosophy of the covenant run." The chapter itself refers to the philosophy and idea of the covenant as "spiritual commercialism" and summarizes the Puritan conception of it as something so binding that, under certain circumstances, "we may go to God and *demand* our salvation of Him" (p. 389). A few pages later it again summarizes: "By dealing through a covenant, God is able to present His case so that no man of ordinary intelligence should continue unconverted, if only on the grounds of self-interest." The words in *The Sincere Convert* which seem pertinent to the matter are under the general heading "Now there are nine easy ways to Heaven, (as men think) all which lead to Hell" (p. 105) and are as follows: "Ninthly, and lastly, the way of *Self-love*,

whereby a man fearing terribly he shall be damned, useth dil-ligently all means whereby he shall be saved. Here is the strong-est difficulty of all, to row against the stream, and to hate a man's self, and then to follow Christ fully" (pp. 109–10). I am not sure, however, that this is a fair illustration of the danger in applying "modern habits of thinking" to an interpretation of the works of the Puritans, for Professor Miller's own logic is more difficult to follow than is that of most writers dealing with the seventeenth century.

28. Abraham Fraunce, for example, in *The Lawiers Logike* (Lon-don, 1588), bk. 1, chap. 3, named the genus of the efficient and material as "the cause before the thing caused" and in a number of other respects expounded the Ramean system in a way that Milton did not follow. Milton himself, in an afterthought con-cerning the "impulsive cause," thought that it might be consid-ered more properly under the efficient in one of its third rather than second modes of working (p. 41).

Checklist of Publications:
1930–1982

I
Books

1. *The Connecticut Wits.* Chicago: University of Chicago Press, 1941.
2. *Herman Melville: A Biography.* Berkeley and Los Angeles: University of California Press, 1951.
3. *Victorian Knight-Errant: A Study of the Early Literary Career of James Russell Lowell.* Berkeley and Los Angeles: University of California Press, 1952.
4. *Literature and the American Tradition.* Garden City: Doubleday & Co., 1960.
5. *"The Mind" of Jonathan Edwards: A Reconstructed Text.* Berkeley and Los Angeles: University of California Press (University of California English Studies: 28), 1963.

II
Pamphlets

1. *The Vision of Joel Barlow.* Los Angeles: The Grey Bow Press, 1937.
2. "The Puritans in Old and New England," pp. 1–25 in *Anglo-American Cultural Relations in the Seventeenth and Eighteenth Centuries.* Los Angeles: William Andrews Clark Memorial Library, 1958.

3. *Herman Melville*. Minneapolis: University of Minnesota Press, 1961.
4. *The Logic of Hamlet's Soliloquies*. Copenhagen: The Lone Pine Press, 1964.
5. *Wright Morris*. Minneapolis: University of Minnesota Press, 1968.

III
Introductions to
Books and Pamphlets

1. Philip Pain, *Daily Meditations*. San Marino: Henry E. Huntington Library and Art Gallery, 1936.
2. Herman Melville, *Moby-Dick*. New York: The Modern Library, 1950.
3. John Phillips, *A Satyre Against Hypocrites*. Los Angeles: William Andrews Clark Memorial Library (The Augustan Reprint Society), 1953.
4. Foreword to *American History in the Novel, 1585–1900*, reprinted from *The Midwest Journal* 8 (Spring–Fall 1956): 374–406.
5. James Fenimore Cooper, *The Pioneers*. New York: Rinehart & Co., 1959.

IV
Essays in Books

1. "Americanization of the European Heritage," in *The American Writer and the European Tradition*, ed. Margaret Denny and William H. Gilman. Minneapolis: University of Minnesota Press, 1950, pp. 78–89.
2. "The Late Eighteenth Century: An Age of Contradictions," in *Transitions in American Literary History*, ed. Harry H. Clark. Durham: Duke University Press, 1953, pp. 49–90.
3. "Herman Melville," in *Eight American Writers*, ed. Norman Foerster and Robert P. Falk. New York: W. W. Norton & Co., 1963, pp. 781–95.
4. "Herman Melville, *Moby-Dick*," in *The American Novel*, ed. Wallace Stegner. New York: Basic Books, 1965, pp. 25–34.

5. "The Mystery of Melville's Short Stories," in *Americana-Austriaca*, ed. Klaus Lanzinger (Festschrift des Amerika-Institus der Universitat Innsbruck). Wien-Stuttgart: Wilhelm Braumuller, 1966, pp. 204–16.
6. "Historical Note" on *Typee* in the Newberry-Northwestern edition of *The Writings of Herman Melville*, I. Evanston: Northwestern University Press, 1967, pp. 277–302.
7. "Herman Melville," in *Six American Novelists*, ed. Richard Foster. Minneapolis: University of Minnesota Press, 1968, pp. 82–117.
8. Section I of the "Historical Note" on *Pierre* in the Newberry-Northwestern edition of *The Writings of Herman Melville*, 7. Evanston: Northwestern University Press, 1971, pp. 365–79.
9. "Poe's *Eureka:* The Detective Story That Failed," in *The Mystery and Detection Annual*, ed. Donald Adams. Beverley Hills: Donald Adams, 1972, pp. 1–14.
10. "The Puritans in Old and New England," in *Stuart and Georgian Moments*, ed. Earl Miner. Berkeley: University of California Press, 1972, pp. 47–71.
11. "Raymond Chandler's Not-so-Great Gatsby," in *Mystery and Detection Annual*, ed. Donald Adams. Beverley Hills: Donald Adams, 1973, pp. 1–15.
12. "Melville and the American Tragic Hero," in *Four Makers of the American Mind*, ed. Thomas Crawley. Durham: Duke University Press, 1976, pp. 65–82.

V
Essays in Periodicals

1. "Towards a Historical Aspect of American Speech Consciousness," *American Speech* 5 (April 1930): 301–5.
2. "Walt Whitman and the American Language," *American Speech* 5 (August 1930): 441–50.
3. "Melville and Spenser—A Note on Criticism," *Modern Language Notes* 46 (May 1931): 291–92.
4. "For a Critique of Whitman's Transcendentalism," *Modern Language Notes* 47 (February 1932): 79–85.
5. "Wordsworth in America," *Modern Language Notes* 48 (June 1933): 359–65.

6. "Figures of Allegory," *The Sewanee Review* 42 (January–March 1934): 54–66.

7. "A Predecessor of Moby-Dick," *Modern Language Notes* 49 (May 1934): 310–11.

8. "Early American Copies of Milton," *The Huntington Library Bulletin* No. 7 (April 1935): 169–79.

9. "The Influence of Milton on Colonial American Poetry," *The Huntington Library Bulletin* No. 9 (April 1936): 63–89.

10. "Joel Barlow and Napoleon," *The Huntington Library Quarterly* 2 (October 1938): 37–51.

11. "Thomas Odiorne: An American Predecessor of Wordsworth," *American Literature* 10 (January 1939): 417–36.

12. "Literature and the Frontier: The Case of Sally Hastings," *ELH, A Journal of English Literary History* 7 (March 1940): 68–82.

13. "Melville's Struggle with the Angel," *Modern Language Quarterly* 1 (June 1940): 195–206. Reprinted in *The Recognition of Herman Melville,* ed. Hershel Parker. Ann Arbor: University of Michigan Press, 1967.

14. "Replies to Reviewers," *American Literature* 16 (November 1944): 226–34.

15. "'The Invention' of Milton's 'Great Argument': A Study of the Logic of 'God's Ways to Men,'" *The Huntington Library Quarterly* 9 (February 1946): 149–73.

16. "The American Revolt Against Pope," *Studies in Philology* 49 (January 1952): 48–65.

17. "'That Two-Handed Engine' Once More," *The Huntington Library Quarterly* 15 (February 1952): 173–84.

18. "Hawthorne's Fiction," *Nineteenth-Century Fiction* 7 (March 1953): 237–50.

19. "Shakespeare for the Family," *The Quarterly of Film, Radio, and Television* 8 (Summer 1954): 356–66.

20. "The Case of the Missing Whaler," *Manuscripts* 12 (Fall 1960): 3–9.

21. "The Case of the Sanded Signature," *Manuscripts* 13 (Spring 1961): 13–17.

22. "Requiem for the Champ" (Hemingway), *The Johns Hopkins Magazine* (October 1961): 10–11, 24–26.

23. "The Creative Imagination of a College Rebel: Jonathan Edwards' Undergraduate Writing," *Early American Literature* 5 (January 1971): 50–56.

24. "Portia's Reasoning in the Trial Scene of Shakespeare's *The Merchant of Venice*," *Neuphilologische Mitteilungen* 48 (Helsinki, 1972): 103–9.
25. "Clarel's Pilgrimage and the Calendar," *Extracts* (Melville Society Newsletter), No. 16 (November 1973): 2–3.
26. "Carlyle and the Conclusion of *Moby-Dick*" (with James Barbour), *The New England Quarterly* 49 (June 1976): 214–24.
27. "The Composition of *The Sound and the Fury*," with "Twilight" (a possible story of William Faulkner's as reconstituted by Leon Howard from *The Sound and the Fury*), *The Missouri Review* 5 (Winter 1981–82): 111–38.

VI
For Limited Circulation

1. *Innocence, Sense, and Nonsense* (facsimile reprints of "The Little Professor," occasional column in the *Los Angeles Times*, opposite the editorial page, from 1953 through 1959). Albuquerque, 1973.
2. Mysteries and Manuscripts (reprints of V. 20 with six additional essays: "The Case of the Off-Color Envelopes," "The Case of the Left-Out Letter," "The Case of the Made-Up Manuscript," "The Case of the Orphaned Poems," "The Case of the Lurid Love," and "A Case of Conscience"). Albuquerque, 1976.
3. *Renaissance Uses of Ramean Logic* (reprints of II. 4, and V. 15 and 24, with two additional essays on "Ramean Hermeneutics and the Commandment Against Adultery," and "A Lawyer's Light on Legal Logic"). Albuquerque, 1977.

VII
Papers for Limited Circulation
Outside the United States

1. "The Long Foreground of Whitman's *Leaves of Grass*" (Mimeograph: Tokyo University, 1954).
2. "The Position of the Intellectual in the Society of the United States" (Mimeograph: Lund University, 1960).
3. "The 'Hard-boiled' School in American Fiction—From the

'Lost' to the 'Beat' Generation" (Mimeograph: Stockholm School of Econmics, 1960).

4. "Herman Melville's *Moby-Dick*" (printed pamphlet: Voice of America Forum Lectures, 1964. U.S. reprint IV. 4).

VII
Miscellaneous

1. Occasional reviews in *Modern Language Notes, Modern Language Quarterly, American Literature, Virginia Quarterly Review, Nineteenth-Century Fiction, Western Folklore,* the *Los Angeles Times,* and the *Mississippi Valley Historical Review.*

2. Various pieces on international, literary, educational, and other subjects in the *Los Angeles Times,* opposite the editorial pages, on the following dates: 1953—January 23, 30; February 9, 15, 27; March 6, 19, 29; April 2, 8, 15, 24; May 10; June 11, 21; July 15; August 9, 20; September 27; October 11 (abbreviated and reprinted in various literary journals and the *Democratic Digest*), 30; November 3; 1954—January 17, 21; March, n.r.; May 21, 25; June 1, 6, 16, 23; August 18; September 2, 22; November 1; 1955—April 28; June 23, 29; July 6, 11, 15, 21, 26; August 3, 8; September 9; October 14, 18, 24, 28; November 3, 10, 28; December 6, 12, 14; 1956—January 24; February 1, 21; May 6, 10, 18; June 1; July 13; August 17; November 13, 20; December 10, 20; 1957—January 10, 11, 24; February 7, 14; March 5; November 21, 24; December 13, 24; 1958—January 9; May 7, 8; July 11, 27; August 12, 20, 28; 1959 (in Sunday book section)—March 8, 15 (cf. California Association of Teachers of English, 1960 Proceedings, pp. 26–29). Collected and published in *Innocence, Sense, and Nonsense* (VI–1).

3. Various articles in the *Encyclopedia Britannica* and *Colliers Encyclopedia.*

IX
Publications
in Foreign Languages

1. "Society and the Individual in 20th Century American Lit-

erature" (Japanese translation by Norihero Nabeshima), in *The Contemporary American Outlook*. Tokyo: Tokyo University Press, 1954, pp. 31–51.

2. Introduction to *Moby-Dick* (Yugoslav translation of III–2). Zagreb: Kultura, 1954.

3. "Die Entstehung von 'Moby-Dick,'" in *Zwei Völker im Gespräch*. Frankfurt am Main: Europäische Verlagsanstalt, 1961, pp. 146–56.

4. "Herman Melville," in *Tres Escritores Nortea Americanos* (Spanish translation II–3). Madrid: Editorial Gredos, 1962, pp. 7–54.

5. *Herman Melville* (Portuguese translation of II–3). Sao Paulo: Livaria Martins Editora, 1963.

6. *Herman Melville* (Arabic translation of II–3). Beirut: Al Maktaba Al Ahliyya, 1963.

7. *La Literatura y la Tradicion Norteamericana* (Spanish translation of I–4). Mexico City: Editorial Novaro Mexico, 1964.

8. *A Literatura Norte-Americana* (Portuguese translation of I–4). Sao Paulo: Editora Cultrix, 1964.

9. *Herman Melville* (Korean translation of II–3 with parallel English text). Seoul: English Literary Society of Korea, 1964.

10. "Herman Melville," in *Series of American Authors*, Vol. III (Japanese translation of II–3), Tokyo: Hokuseido, 1964, pp. 139–93.

11. *Literature and the American Tradition* (Japanese translation of I–4). Tokyo: Shinozaki Shorin, 1968.

·

Index

.